Mexico

Other Books of Related Interest:

Opposing Viewpoints Series

The Catholic Church

Church and State

Illegal Immigration

The US Latino Community

At Issue Series

How Does Religion Influence Politics?

Should the US Be Multilingual?

Should the US Close Its Borders?

Should There Be an International Climate Treaty?

Current Controversies Series

Drug Legalization

Fair Trade

Immigration

"Congress shall make no law . . . abridging the freedom of speech, or of the press."

First Amendment to the US Constitution

The basic foundation of our democracy is the First Amendment guarantee of freedom of expression. The Opposing Viewpoints series is dedicated to the concept of this basic freedom and the idea that it is more important to practice it than to enshrine it.

OPPOSING
VIEWPOINTS®
SERIES

| Mexico

David Haugen and Susan Musser, Book Editors

GREENHAVEN PRESS
A part of Gale, Cengage Learning

GALE
CENGAGE Learning™

Detroit • New York • San Francisco • New Haven, Conn • Waterville, Maine • London

Elizabeth Des Chenes, *Managing Editor*

© 2012 Greenhaven Press, a part of Gale, Cengage Learning

Gale and Greenhaven Press are registered trademarks used herein under license.

For more information, contact:
Greenhaven Press
27500 Drake Rd.
Farmington Hills, MI 48331-3535
Or you can visit our Internet site at gale.cengage.com

For product information and technology assistance, contact us at

Gale Customer Support, 1-800-877-4253
For permission to use material from this text or product, submit all requests online at www.cengage.com/permissions

Further permissions questions can be emailed to permissionrequest@cengage.com

Articles in Greenhaven Press anthologies are often edited for length to meet page requirements. In addition, original titles of these works are changed to clearly present the main thesis and to explicitly indicate the author's opinion. Every effort is made to ensure that Greenhaven Press accurately reflects the original intent of the authors. Every effort has been made to trace the owners of copyrighted material.

Cover image copyright © David Frazier/Corbis.

LIBRARY OF CONGRESS CATALOGING-IN-PUBLICATION DATA

Mexico / David Haugen and Susan Musser, book editors.
    p. cm. -- (Opposing viewpoints)
    Includes bibliographical references and index.
    ISBN 978-0-7377-5737-8 (hardcover) -- ISBN 978-0-7377-5738-5 (pbk.)
    1. Social problems--Mexico. 2. Mexico--Social conditions--1970- 3. Mexico--Emigration and immigration. 4. United States--Foreign economic relations--Mexico. 5. Mexico--Foreign economc relations--United States. I. Haugen, David M., 1969- II. Musser, Susan.
    HN117.M487 2011
    306.0972'09051--dc22

                                      2011013476

Printed in the United States of America
1 2 3 4 5 6 7 15 14 13 12 11

Contents

Chapter 3: Is Cross-Border Migration a Problem for the United States and Mexico?

Chapter 4: What Should US Policy Be Toward Mexico?

Why Consider Opposing Viewpoints?

> "The only way in which a human being can make some approach to knowing the whole of a subject is by hearing what can be said about it by persons of every variety of opinion and studying all modes in which it can be looked at by every character of mind. No wise man ever acquired his wisdom in any mode but this."
>
> *John Stuart Mill*

In our media-intensive culture it is not difficult to find differing opinions. Thousands of newspapers and magazines and dozens of radio and television talk shows resound with differing points of view. The difficulty lies in deciding which opinion to agree with and which "experts" seem the most credible. The more inundated we become with differing opinions and claims, the more essential it is to hone critical reading and thinking skills to evaluate these ideas. Opposing Viewpoints books address this problem directly by presenting stimulating debates that can be used to enhance and teach these skills. The varied opinions contained in each book examine many different aspects of a single issue. While examining these conveniently edited opposing views, readers can develop critical thinking skills such as the ability to compare and contrast authors' credibility, facts, argumentation styles, use of persuasive techniques, and other stylistic tools. In short, the Opposing Viewpoints Series is an ideal way to attain the higher-level thinking and reading skills so essential in a culture of diverse and contradictory opinions.

In addition to providing a tool for critical thinking, Opposing Viewpoints books challenge readers to question their own strongly held opinions and assumptions. Most people form their opinions on the basis of upbringing, peer pressure, and personal, cultural, or professional bias. By reading carefully balanced opposing views, readers must directly confront new ideas as well as the opinions of those with whom they disagree. This is not to argue simplistically that everyone who reads opposing views will—or should—change his or her opinion. Instead, the series enhances readers' understanding of their own views by encouraging confrontation with opposing ideas. Careful examination of others' views can lead to the readers' understanding of the logical inconsistencies in their own opinions, perspective on why they hold an opinion, and the consideration of the possibility that their opinion requires further evaluation.

Evaluating Other Opinions

To ensure that this type of examination occurs, Opposing Viewpoints books present all types of opinions. Prominent spokespeople on different sides of each issue as well as well-known professionals from many disciplines challenge the reader. An additional goal of the series is to provide a forum for other, less known, or even unpopular viewpoints. The opinion of an ordinary person who has had to make the decision to cut off life support from a terminally ill relative, for example, may be just as valuable and provide just as much insight as a medical ethicist's professional opinion. The editors have two additional purposes in including these less known views. One, the editors encourage readers to respect others' opinions—even when not enhanced by professional credibility. It is only by reading or listening to and objectively evaluating others' ideas that one can determine whether they are worthy of consideration. Two, the inclusion of such viewpoints encourages the important critical thinking skill of objectively evaluating an author's credentials and bias. This evaluation will illuminate an author's reasons for taking a particular stance on an issue and will aid in readers' evaluation of the author's ideas.

It is our hope that these books will give readers a deeper understanding of the issues debated and an appreciation of the complexity of even seemingly simple issues when good and honest people disagree. This awareness is particularly important in a democratic society such as ours in which people enter into public debate to determine the common good. Those with whom one disagrees should not be regarded as enemies but rather as people whose views deserve careful examination and may shed light on one's own.

Thomas Jefferson once said that "difference of opinion leads to inquiry, and inquiry to truth." Jefferson, a broadly educated man, argued that "if a nation expects to be ignorant and free . . . it expects what never was and never will be." As individuals and as a nation, it is imperative that we consider the opinions of others and examine them with skill and discernment. The Opposing Viewpoints Series is intended to help readers achieve this goal.

David L. Bender and Bruno Leone,
Founders

Introduction

> *"My administration's central objective is transforming Mexico. And I call on Mexicans to do this. Transforming Mexico from being a country with almost half of its population in poverty, into being a prosperous, just country where we have eradicated extreme poverty.... From a Mexico threatened by criminality and violence, to a Mexico in peace, a free Mexico, a Mexico in which our children can walk, play, study, grow and live in peace and with dignity. I think of that Mexico and I hold on firmly to the idea that it is possible to have it."*
>
> —*Mexican president Felipe Calderón, State of the Nation address, September 2007*

When Felipe Calderón took over as president of Mexico in 2006, the nation seemed to teeter on the brink of instability. Left-wing politicos argued that the newly elected president had stolen the election, and they vowed to disrupt his policy making; unemployment remained at a stubborn 3.6 percent; the price of corn was skyrocketing beyond the capability of Mexico's poor to pay for their traditional tortillas; and drug cartels fought to control the lucrative trade, leaving violence and corpses in their wake. In a country that had suffered these and similar plagues for nearly a decade, few anticipated significant change under Calderón.

However, the new administration showed alacrity in responding to crises. Writing a special report in April 2007 on the president's first hundred days for the Pacific Council on International Policy, Chappell H. Lawson succinctly noted, "Calderón moved swiftly from his first day in office." The president put caps on rising corn prices, cut government salaries while raising the pay of police officers and soldiers, and began an all-out war against the drug lords by sending sixty-five hundred troops to the midwestern state of Michoacán, where a new "family" was fighting to establish itself. Observers in both Mexico and the United States were surprised to see a president who moved from word to deed so quickly, and some remarked how Mexico, amidst the flurry of activity, had not imploded. Lawson, for one, concluded, "Regional conflicts . . . have not pushed the country into turmoil; protests [by the political opposition] . . . have not turned violent; and political polarization has not destabilized Mexico's democracy."

Calderón's actions, though, have not convinced everyone that Mexico's problems are under control. The drug cartels garner the most publicity both in Mexico and north of the border because continuing inter-cartel slayings and recent assassinations of political officials suggest that the government does not have the drug lords on the run. Following the ambush and killing of Tamaulipas gubernatorial candidate Rodolfo Cantu in July 2010, Calderón stated, "Today has proven that organized crime is a permanent threat and that we should close ranks to confront it and prevent it from repeating acts such as the cowardly assassination that shocked the country today." Despite such rhetoric and the nearly fifty thousand Mexican troops stationed in key states, the killings have not stopped. On January 8, 2011, news services reported that fifteen bodies of young Mexican men were discovered near a shopping mall in the popular resort city of Acapulco where the Sinaloa cartel—one of Mexico's strongest—holds sway. Reuters relayed news that "at least a dozen more bodies were found at several scenes of violence around the city early on [that] Saturday." The ongoing murders have led many to conclude that Calderón's war on drugs is simply fueling more violence. Writing for the *Progressive* on April 1, 2010, Miguel Tinker Salas pointed out, "More than 19,000 Mexicans have died in this failed war, almost four times as many casualties as the United States has suffered in the Iraq and Afghanistan wars combined." The president, however, has stuck to his policy, insisting that the recent capture of drug kingpins proves the worth of his uncompromising strategy. Salas, for one, rejects such optimism, arguing that after each military victory, "the cartels regroup and initiate operations elsewhere so that increasingly all of Mexico feels the pain of this expanding conflict."

The war against the drug lords has overshadowed many of the other social and economic concerns Mexico faces in the second decade of the twenty-first century. The nation's economy has been a focal point of criticism for years because many believe the lack of opportunities is helping the drug lords recruit more idle workers. According to the US Department of State, around 44 percent of the population lives below the poverty line, and good-paying jobs are scarce. Opening its doors to US imports under the North American Free Trade Agreement (NAFTA) has devastated the agricultural sector while creating relatively few jobs in maquiladoras, satellite manufacturing plants that assemble products for companies in the United States. Mexico has placed its faith in globalization, but the transition is still beset by growing pains. For example, although Mexico can offer cheap labor, it cannot match the inexpensive labor force in China, and thus Mexico cannot fully take advantage of its strong worker base. Still, the country expects growth in gross domestic product of about 4 percent in 2011, and various industries such as clothing manufacturing are still booming because of the close proximity to apparel businesses in the United States.

One of the nation's biggest economic concerns, though, is its oil revenues. Filling 40 percent of the federal budgetary income, the oil industry (Pemex) in Mexico is state run and has, until recently, rejected foreign investment and exploration. In an article for the Politico web magazine dated May 20, 2010, Roger Pardo-Maurer bemoans the monopoly and its restrictions on new drilling operations. "With yields at key fields now plunging 14 percent annually," Pardo-Maurer writes, "Mexico is projected to become a net oil importer as early as 2017—an extraordinary reversal for the second-largest oil supplier to the United States." In December 2010, the government allowed some private contractors to expand Pemex's operations, and officials hope the move will stave off the date at which Mexico will lose its lucrative global export.

Revenue and employment issues are also affecting Mexican society. Mexico has never maintained a unified culture; its many states are home to sixty-two recognized indigenous peoples as well as ethnic enclaves from past European migrations. The majority of Mexico's Amerindian populations live in the southwestern states (Guerrero, Oaxaca, and Chiapas), where industry is sluggish and poverty is high. According to an October 19, 2010, article by Emilio Godoy for the Inter Press Service (IPS), the United Nations Development Programme reports that 38 percent of Mexico's indigenous people live below the poverty line. Some believe the indigenous people of the south are subjugated and their needs are not met even as their land is stripped of its wealth of natural resources. The Zapatista Army of National Liberation has waged an ongoing "war" in Chiapas since 1994 against what they view as the exploitation of the region. They reject globalization, strive to protect the state's rain forests from reckless lumber practices, and resist Pemex's control of the region's petroleum reserves and the environmental degradation caused by drilling.

Another pressing problem that affects both the economy and society as a whole is the rampant corruption that still pervades Mexico's government, military, and police. Of primary concern is the number of officials and law enforcement personnel in the pay of the drug cartels. In early 2010, nearly two dozen mayors and other officials were arrested in the state of Michoacán alone on charges of bribery and covering up drug trafficking. By the end of the year, Mexico had fired about 10 percent of its federal police forces on corruption allegations. Some deplore the level of corruption in Mexico, but others are more sympathetic, knowing that public officials who stand up to the drug lords jeopardize the safety of their families and themselves. Writing for the *Wall Street Journal* on January 16, 2009, Joel Kurtzman attests that Mexico has always considered corruption part of the status quo: "Everyone knew a large number of government officials were taking bribes, but no one did anything about it." Such an attitude, in Kurtzman's view, makes it difficult for Mexicans and outsiders to "tell the good guys from the bad," implying that if Mexico cannot clean up its governing institutions, instability could tear the nation apart.

The Calderón administration has pledged to continue its fight against the cartels and the corrupt officials in their pay, and for some observers, this commitment as well as Mexico's trend toward expanding democracy suggest that Mexico will not become a failed state. Teo Molin, an intern at *Human Events* magazine, wrote a piece for the journal's website on June 1, 2009, in which he maintained, "Mexico is still sovereign, and has an active economy and operational federal government in most of its territory." Therefore, writing Mexico off as a failed state is, in his view, "a stretch." In *Opposing Viewpoints: Mexico*, various foreign policy analysts, political and economic experts, and other interested commentators examine the problems Mexico faces in the twenty-first century and argue whether the government can respond to them effectively. In the opening chapter, What Is Contributing to the Instability of Mexican Society? these observers directly address the influence and impact of the criminal, economic, and political factors that have caused some to worry that Mexico is failing. In the remaining chapters titled What Has Been the Impact of NAFTA on Mexico? Is Cross-Border Migration a Problem for the United States and Mexico? and What Should US Policy Be Toward Mexico? other experts debate the reforms and political strategies the Mexican government and the US government have employed and should employ to propel the nation forward on its path toward greater social justice and economic achievement. Whether such growth is likely in the next few years is still a point of contention, but Mexico has proved itself capable in the past of overcoming economic crises and creating more democratic and transparent institutions. As President Calderón remarked in his 2007 State of the Nation address, "Today, democracy provides us with the opportunity to build a nation where we all live better. Let us build together a Mexico that lives up to our history, up to our times, our challenges, our dreams, a Mexico that lives up to our dignity." The Mexican people's hopes are tied to this spirit of determination; all that remains is to ensure that word turns into deed.

CHAPTER 1

What Is Contributing to the Instability of Mexican Society?

Chapter Preface

In a February 12, 2009, Heritage Foundation web memo on Mexico's growing instability, international trade and policy analysts James M. Roberts and Ray Walser begin their examination by stating, "Drug-related crime and rampant violence have battered Mexico's sense of public security and confidence in the government's capacity to protect the lives of its citizens." The assessment is not unique; many journalists and analysts have pronounced the same judgment over the last few years. Like Roberts and Walser, most fix the blame for Mexico's social insecurity on the power and murderous capabilities of Mexico's drug cartels, related political and police corruption, and the government's inability to root out the entrenched drug lords and their armies. American observers fear that if these problems are not rectified or at least controlled, violence could spill over the border and transnational trade will suffer.

For some in the United States and in Mexico, the election of President Felipe Calderón signaled a promising turn in the fight against the drug cartels. His predecessor, Vicente Fox, had sent small numbers of troops to Mexican states along the Rio Grande, but several politicians and reporters on both sides of the border thought the effort was halfhearted and poorly executed. When Calderón took office in 2006, he mobilized large sections of the army to put down the drug-related violence in key states. In a January 23, 2007, interview in Britain's *Financial Times*, Calderón stated, "Since we started these operations we have received very encouraging results. In the state of Michoacán [on Mexico's central Pacific coast], for example, the murder rate has fallen almost 40 percent compared with the average over the last six months. People's support in the regions where we are operating has grown, and that has been very important. Opinion polls have confirmed that, and I think we have made it clear to everyone that this issue is a priority for us." Over time, though, the roughly fifty thousand troops Calderón committed to the fight have been bogged down in street battles in various cities owned by the drug trade. Failing to adapt quickly, the army resorted to procedures it knew well. As Tracy Wilkinson and Ken Ellingwood reported to the *Los Angeles Times* on December 29, 2010, "The army . . . has frequently fallen back on time-worn tactics, such as highway checkpoints, that are of limited use against drug traffickers, especially in cities."

Given the military's "limited" success, President Calderón became more vociferous in accusing the United States of exacerbating Mexico's problems. In a speech delivered to the Mexican people on June 16, 2010, Calderón called the United States "the world's largest drug consumer" and criticized Mexico's neighbor for lifting a ban on assault weapons in 2004, making it "very easy for criminal groups to purchase powerful weapons in the US and bring them to Mexico for criminal purposes." US pundits, however, have pointed out that the type of weaponry seized from drug cartels clearly is more powerful than the rifles sold at US gun shows. Some US critics and Mexican politicians have also spoken up about complaints against the Mexican army for alleged human rights violations in the regions now patrolled. Thousands of civil complaints have been recorded in various Mexican states since 2006, accusing soldiers of engaging in torture, theft, rape, and murder. Calderón has stated that all legitimate complaints are being prosecuted, but various human rights organizations claim abuses regularly go unpunished, proving that the drug war is failing the Mexican people in more than just its lackluster performance in stopping the narcotics trade and the cartel-sponsored violence.

In the chapter that follows, several commentators offer their opinions on Mexico's pressing problems and whether Mexico's political leadership and US cross-border policies are helping or hindering their resolution.

> "[Mexican drug cartels'] efficient orga-
> nization allows them to leverage fire-
> power and money on a scale large
> enough to threaten the state."

Mexican Drug Cartels Are Destabilizing Democracy in Mexico

Mario Loyola

In the viewpoint that follows, Mario Loyola, a contributor to the National Review, the Weekly Standard, *and other newsmagazines, describes the power and influence of the drug cartels headquartered in Mexico. According to Loyola, the drug lords have both political influence and military muscle, making them difficult foes for Mexican authorities to dislodge. He maintains that the Mexican government's efforts have focused on rooting out police and administrative corruption that have tarnished Mexican democracy and proven just how disunified the state authority remains. More significantly, Loyola praises Mexico's efforts to forge a partnership with the United States to break up distribution networks and lower demand for drugs. Although Loyola asserts that these activities have yielded some positive results, he warns that the cartels are well established, well connected, and*

Mario Loyola, "Mexico's Cartel Wars," *National Review*, vol. 61, June 22, 2009. Copyright © 2009 by National Review, Inc. Reproduced by permission.

*even well liked in various Mexican states and will continue to
fight a bloody war to keep their illicit economy going.*

As you read, consider the following questions:

1. As Loyola defines them, who are the Zetas and what
   background do many of them share?

2. Joaquín "El Chapo" Guzmán reportedly heads which
   Mexican drug cartel, according to the author?

3. As Loyola reports, how has the Calderón government
   tried to increase the trustworthiness and loyalty of the
   Mexican police force?

Archbishop Héctor González caused a mini-scandal in
Mexico when he declared recently that the country's most
notorious drug baron, Joaquín "El Chapo" ("The Kid")
Guzmán, was living right outside a small town in the
archbishop's home state of Durango, and that "everyone except the authorities" knew it. No sooner had González apolo-
gized for what one commentator called an irresponsible "dif-
fusion of gossip" than the bodies of two military-intelligence
officers on an undercover surveillance operation turned up
right where the archbishop had indicated, riddled with bullets
from high-powered rifles. The bodies bore a characteristic
warning: "Neither government nor priests will ever be able to
take on El Chapo."

It's not an idle boast. Even the Pentagon has started to
worry. Noting that Mexico's governing institutions "are all under sustained assault and pressure by criminal gangs and drug
cartels," one recent [U.S.] Joint Forces Command study warned
of the "serious implications for homeland security" of "any
descent by Mexico into chaos."

A Nation of Progress and Despair

Ironically, Mexico's struggle against the cartels is both a symptom and a symbol of the country's increasingly successful

march to modernity and affluence. After 15 years of steady growth, Mexico's GDP [gross domestic product] per capita is now the highest in Latin America (and five times that of China), while unemployment is the lowest in the OECD [Organisation for Economic Co-operation and Development]. Today's Mexico bears little resemblance to the country I visited 20 years ago. Here in Mexico City, packed bars and restaurants abound, and commerce seems frenetic. Cities such as Monterrey are brimming with industry, shopping malls, and Wal-Marts. But in other parts of Mexico, where drug cartels battle for control of trafficking routes and bases of operation, violence is rife, the streets are deserted, and entire police forces have disintegrated. With official corruption still ubiquitous, Mexicans have little confidence in their government, or in the rule of law.

Pres. Felipe Calderón has staked his legacy on changing that mentality—and we have a lot riding on his success. To protect the gains of recent decades—and because they truly believe that Mexico can achieve first-world status—Calderón and his predecessor, Vicente Fox, refused to turn a blind eye to the drug trade as prior governments had done. Fox began prosecuting corrupt senior officials rather than merely pushing them out of their positions, and abandoned a policy against extraditions to the United States. Calderón has gone further: From his first days in office, he has made crushing the cartels and ridding the government of corruption the focus of his administration.

The results have been bloody. As cartel leaders have been captured and killed, exceedingly violent power struggles have ensued. According to Juan Zarate, Pres. George W. Bush's deputy national security adviser for counterterrorism, the cartels' battle for control of key trafficking routes is terrorizing border cities like Tijuana and Juárez. There were nearly 6,000 drug-related assassinations in Mexico last year [2008], about double the prior year's number, heavily concentrated in areas where cartels clash. The vast majority of the victims were cartel members, but perhaps 10 percent were law enforcement and government officials. As police forces are vetted and purged of corrupt elements, the cartels are forced to switch from bribery to intimidation, murder, and terrorism to keep them at bay.

The Power of the Cartels

Reducing drug use and even drug trafficking are, in a sense, secondary goals of Mexico's drug war. The main goal is to break up the cartels themselves. The reason is simple: Their efficient organization allows them to leverage firepower and money on a scale large enough to threaten the state. But they have been hit hard by the government's offensive: Most of their founding members are now dead or in prison, and in many cases, top-down leadership has disappeared altogether, giving way to atomized, horizontal structures, fleeting alliances, and chronic intramural conflict.

Most accounts put the number of Mexico's major drug cartels at five or six. Each is thought to be based in a particular town or region, but they are present at production sources throughout Latin America and have distribution networks across the U.S. market.

Part of what has made the cartels so dangerous is their progressive militarization. The best example is the Gulf cartel, which, along with its paramilitary wing, the infamous Zetas, is thought to be the best-armed and most dangerous in Mexico. Years ago, a senior Mexican army officer disappeared and began recruiting Zetas from among Mexico's military. The Zetas have developed the sort of platoon- and company-size tactical operations that one associates with full-blown insurgencies. They use these tactics to battle law enforcement agents and army troops, destroy rival cartels, and murder, kidnap, or intimidate citizens who oppose them, including journalists.

A dizzying array of military firepower has been seized from this organization, including antitank rockets, rocket-propelled grenade launchers, and hundreds of grenades and assault rifles. But after two of its leaders were captured and extradited to the U.S. in rapid succession, the cartel appeared to degenerate into a power struggle among perhaps eight different drug barons, several of whom have been captured or killed. Meanwhile, attrition has sapped the Zetas of their best-trained and most disciplined cadres.

Law Enforcement's Uphill Struggle

At the same time, however, the cartels have managed, through a combination of intimidation and corruption, to bring about the disintegration of entire law enforcement agencies. The best example is the Juárez cartel, based across the Rio Grande from El Paso, Texas. Last year, after it threatened to kill an officer every 48 hours until the police chief resigned, the Juárez police force simply fell apart, and Calderón had to send in some 8,000 army soldiers to patrol the streets. According to Juan Zarate, this has helped to break the cycle of corruption, but in many places the city remains a virtual ghost town. Meanwhile, hundreds of thousands of vehicles continue to cross back and forth between Juárez and El Paso every month, leading some in the U.S. to call for closing the border. But this is out of the question: Millions of jobs in both countries depend on cross-border traffic, and the cartels would simply find another way to get in. Indeed, they are already making increased use of the scores of illegal crossing points that have been identified by the Drug Enforcement Administration, which is woefully understaffed at the border.

The worst-hit cartels have responded by diversifying their sources of revenue. In far northwest Mexico, across the border from San Diego, the Tijuana cartel (whose travails were dramatized in the Steven Soderbergh film *Traffic*) has delved into human trafficking, prostitution, and brokering access to corrupt officials. As the territory it controls has shrunk to just the border towns of Tijuana and Mexicali, and as several of its major figures have deserted to other cartels, the resulting carnage has made Tijuana one of Mexico's most violent cities, with more than 1,200 assassinations last year [2008]. At least 300 families there have reported missing persons, and many streets that once teemed with American tourists are now deserted.

One of the core competencies of the cartels is penetrating government institutions, both to secure police protection and to conduct espionage (particularly to keep abreast of ongoing investigations and planned operations). The organization of the Beltrán Leyva brothers—another major cartel—is infamous in this respect; a member of President Calderón's bodyguard was recently indicted on charges of spying for the brothers on a monthly retainer of $100,000. Widely believed to have given El Chapo his start in the crime business, the brothers later reportedly broke with him and displaced his cartel from the Pacific state of Sonora in what one Mexican official described as a "bloodbath." According to a U.S. law enforcement official in Mexico City, this highlights one major result of the drug war: Cartel alliances are no longer rigid or lasting, but rather transactional, dynamic, and often violent.

Cartels Change Organizational Strategy

Another result of Mexico's war on the cartels resembles what happened to [the terrorist group] al-Qaeda after 9/11 [referring to the September 11, 2001, terrorist attacks on the United States]. Having lost much of their senior leadership, the cartels have reduced their vertical integration, adopting a more fluid horizontal model—a system of autonomous franchises that maintain mutual isolation for greater protection. The cartel that has managed this transition most effectively is the one widely seen to be Mexico's most powerful: the Sinaloa "Federation" of Joaquín "El Chapo" Guzmán.

This cartel is based in the Pacific Coast state of Sinaloa; in combination with a few nearby affiliated organizations, chiefly the "Family" of Michoacán, it is also referred to as the "Pacific cartel." According to Mexican law enforcement officials, the Sinaloa cartel has the most resilient structure of any cartel in Mexico and has managed to secure the best police and military protection in its areas of operation, which run from northern Mexico to the Yucatán Peninsula and Chiapas. It is present throughout the Western Hemisphere, from Argentina, Peru, and Colombia to the U.S. and even Canada. Last February, a massive raid against the cartel by U.S. law enforcement agencies—dubbed "Operation Xcellerator"—netted some 750 arrests of Sinaloa foot soldiers in 26 states across America.

Despite the beating they have taken, Mexico's drug cartels remain entrenched, well armed, and fantastically well financed. Last year, hundreds of millions of dollars were seized from the cartels, more than the U.S. Congress appropriated for counternarcotics efforts in Mexico. This year, El Chapo made it onto *Forbes*'s list of the world's richest people (in an absurd touch, *Forbes* lists his industry as "shipping").

The outcome of Calderón's fight against the cartels remains very much in doubt—at least in the near term—and things could get much worse before they get better. According to one former Bush administration official, the cartels may soon be able to "buy themselves an election" in Mexico, bringing to power an anti-American government tolerant of their activities and friendly to Venezuelan strongman Hugo Chávez.

On the other hand, the situation in Mexico today is not nearly as bad as the situation that faced Colombia ten years ago, when, according to the former Bush official, "the FARC [Revolutionary Armed Forces of Colombia] was in a position to march on Bogotá" and the country was on the verge of becoming a narco-state. Presidential candidates were on the take and vulnerable to assassination, and they could be kidnapped with impunity: Consider the case of Ingrid Betancourt, who was held captive for more than six years in dense jungle. As Juan Zarate points out, the FARC controlled large swathes of jungle territory, and that jungle is one main difference between Colombia and Mexico: Impassable rain forest, which takes up about half the country, provided effective cover for terrorists and other criminal organizations. But in Mexico, according to one U.S. law enforcement official, the difficulty of accessing remote areas is mostly logistical. Not many parts of the country are impassable, so a few advanced helicopters can make a big difference.

Helicopters have been the most high-profile element of the assistance the U.S. is providing to Mexico under the Bush administration's Mérida Initiative [a U.S.-Mexican plan to cooperatively curb drug supply and demand], which President [Barack] Obama has wisely embraced. The program has been compared to Plan Colombia, which helped that nation survive its years of civil turmoil, but a more apt comparison is to the "partnership capacity building" efforts that have guided U.S. policy in the War on Terror. The basic idea of "partnership capacity building" (a term coined by Douglas Feith, the former undersecretary of defense for policy) is to ensure that partner governments are able to govern all of their sovereign territory. As we learned on 9/11, transnational threats thrive in weakly governed or ungoverned areas.

The policy consists of helping nations where transnational terrorist and criminal networks are present to build lawful and effective governance. Areas of assistance range from the military and law enforcement to legislation and even budget administration. As the phrase "partnership" implies, the U.S. seeks to build connections between its institutions and those of its partners. The idea of the Mérida Initiative is not to put U.S. personnel on the ground—as happened in Plan Colombia—but rather to help Mexico become fully effective in our common struggle against drug traffickers. According to one U.S. official in Mexico City, the Mérida Initiative has greatly

Similarities Between US Involvement in Iraq and Mexico

The similarities go a long way. Like Iraq, which is rich in oil, Mexico is rich in drugs (either as producer or transporter), and the biggest market for these commodities is in the United States. Both oil and illegal drugs are imported from countries that struggle with unstable political systems. And now, because of a battle for control of the market—either to own the biggest percentage of the flow or to shut it down—we are in a drug war, just as we have found ourselves in a war for oil.

Sito Negron, "Baghdad, Mexico," Texas Monthly, January 2009. www.texasmonthly.com.

changed the character of cooperation between the U.S. and Mexico. And the cooperation goes both ways: Mexican law enforcement personnel are now sometimes embedded with U.S. agents hunting drug traffickers in the southern U.S., to help the agents understand what they are looking at.

Government Corruption Must Be Overcome

But to be successful, such efforts require a steadfast commitment throughout the institutions of the partner nation. And while Calderón's commitment is not in doubt, the scale of corruption in Mexico leaves a great deal of doubt about the rest of his government. The large number of senior officials under indictment for corruption and drug trafficking, including a former drug czar and a former federal police chief, is both good news and bad news. The good news is that they are being investigated, prosecuted, and punished; the bad news is that so many of them are corrupt in the first place. But with vetting programs such as "Operation Cleanup," Calderón has made the fight against corruption a centerpiece of his administration. A few weeks ago [May of 2009], ten mayors were among dozens of officials arrested on drug-related charges in a single operation. Both the drug barons and the government officials in their pockets are visibly losing their "untouchable" mystique.

Another promising new effort is Plataforma México, an integrated law enforcement network and database that will provide real-time intelligence to local, state, and federal law enforcement. Under the umbrella of the Mérida Initiative, the U.S. has furnished powerful computer servers, and a variety of U.S. agencies are assisting the effort. Perhaps even more important in the long run is a sweeping court reform that will replace Mexico's antiquated and corruption-prone criminal justice system with modern American-style criminal procedures.

The greatest challenges, however, remain local. While the national government is increasingly modern and effective, state and municipal governments remain ensnared in a culture of patronage that is resistant to reform and susceptible to corruption. In the southern state of Chiapas, one young resident of the beautiful town of San Cristóbal tells me that during her few years working in the town government, she was horrified at the extent of corruption—starting with that of the mayor, who would routinely instruct her to sign dubious requests for project funds from favored officials, even when it was clear that the project was merely a cover for graft. Calderón wants public office to be seen as a public service, but in Mexico it is still all too often seen as a lucrative asset.

The town of San Pedro—the Beverly Hills of Monterrey—is emerging as a leader in the effort to forge modern municipal government. While visiting Monterrey, I had several opportunities to meet with San Pedro's mayor, former senator Fernando Margáin, who was chairman of the Mexican senate's foreign relations committee during the presidency of Vicente Fox. He tells me that after the town's police chief was assassinated two years ago, local authorities visited the U.S., as well as several countries in Europe and the Middle East, to survey law enforcement technologies and "best practices."

Out of that effort came a modern "C4" (command, control, communications, and computers) center, which integrates images and communications from fixed surveillance cameras—as well as cameras onboard new American-style police vehicles—in a heavily armored building that can continue to function even if cut off from outside sources of electricity and water. Perhaps more important, half the members of the police force were let go after vetting, and the remainder were retrained while their wages were almost doubled—a policy that has also been used to good effect in Iraq. New recruits have to go through extensive background checks and must submit to routine lie-detector tests. Fernando Margáin reports that theft and other violent crime has plummeted in San Pedro, though drug trafficking has not fallen quite as far.

The Troublesome Image of Drug Lords as Popular Heroes

But there is a long road ahead. After one San Pedro police officer was assassinated in a gangland shooting, Margáin made a statement on television slamming the drug cartels as cowards and killers of innocent people. As he was driving home a short while later, his cell phone rang. "We are not cowards," the voice on the other end said. "We don't kill women or children. Why don't you just let us work?" Mexican drug traffickers are surprisingly touchy about their reputations: Many view themselves as almost romantic figures, men of principle and property and even philanthropic inclinations. The lavish and faintly grotesque mausoleums they provide for themselves and their dearly departed receive visitors regularly, often daily. Like

Pablo Escobar, the Colombian drug lord who was killed in 1993, some drug barons are local heroes.

This may seem quaint, but it is one more way that the cartels pose a deadly threat to Mexican society. As long as cartel members are respected, the state's grip on legitimacy is weakened. Iraq and Afghanistan face similar problems, as did the United States itself in the days of the Wild West. Today we romanticize the outlaws of Sam Peckinpah's *The Wild Bunch*, but it was a good and necessary thing that modernity closed in on them and swept them from the land.

The day before I arrived in Mexico, 44 members of the upper echelon of the Michoacán "Family" were arrested in church while attending a baptism. Once again, operational security was preserved, the suspects had no warning, and not a shot was fired. The subsequent photo op—which got the intended play on front pages across Mexico—seemed staged to deliver a message: The suspects were lined up in handcuffs in front of an imposing police helicopter, as if to symbolize the power of the state. Visible on the engine casing, just above their heads, was a legend both mundane and unmistakably modern: "To Protect and Serve the Community."

*"U.S. policies that help increase account-
ability, expand economic and social opportunity, and strengthen the rule of
law in Mexico will all encourage a
more inclusive and more stable democracy there."*

The United States Must
Support Democracy in Mexico
to Defeat Drug Cartels

Shannon O'Neil

*Shannon O'Neil is a fellow for Latin America studies at the
Council on Foreign Relations, where she presides as director of
the council's task force on US–Latin American relations. In the
following viewpoint, O'Neil portrays the violence surrounding
the drug trade in Mexico as a symptom of the country's growing
middle class and desire for a strong democracy. O'Neil details
many of the political and economic dilemmas that have led to
the maelstrom of bloodshed, but she points out how the Mexican
government under President Felipe Calderón, with the support of
the middle class, has begun to tackle these problems. O'Neil argues that for democracy to survive and succeed against the drug*

Shannon O'Neil, "The Real War in Mexico," *Foreign Affairs*, vol. 88, July–August 2009,
pp. 63–77. Reprinted by permission of Foreign Affairs, July–August 2009. Copyright ©
2009 by the Council on Foreign Relations, Inc. www.ForeignAffairs.com.

cartels, the United States must support Calderón's efforts and create policies to stem drug demand, monitor the border, bolster the Mexican economy, and discourage Mexico's middle class from fleeing to better jobs in America.

As you read, consider the following questions:

1. According to the author, how did the rule of the PRI limit violence between authorities, drug cartels, and civilians?

2. As O'Neil claims, about what percentage of guns seized in Mexico comes from the United States?

3. In the author's opinion, what "paltry" amount of US development aid was sent to Mexico in 2009?

Brazen assassinations, kidnappings, and intimidation by drug lords conjure up images of Colombia in the early 1990s. Yet today it is Mexico that is engulfed by escalating violence. Over 10,000 drug-related killings have occurred since President Felipe Calderón took office in December 2006; in 2008 alone, there were over 6,000. Drug cartels have begun using guerrilla-style tactics: sending heavily armed battalions to attack police stations and assassinating police officers, government officials, and journalists. And they have also adopted innovative public relations strategies to recruit supporters and intimidate their enemies: displaying *narcomantas*—banners hung by drug traffickers—in public places and uploading videos of gruesome beheadings to YouTube.

Washington is just waking up to the violence next door. Last December [2008], the U.S. Joint Forces Command's *Joint Operating Environment, 2008* paired Mexico with Pakistan in its discussion of "worst-case scenarios"—states susceptible to "a rapid and sudden collapse." In January, Michael Hayden, the departing CIA chief, claimed that Mexico could become "more problematic than Iraq," and Michael Chertoff, the departing secretary of homeland security, announced that the Department of Homeland Security has a "contingency plan for border violence, so if we did get a significant spillover, we have a surge—if I may use that word—capability." The U.S. media breathlessly proclaims that Mexico is "on the brink."

This rising hysteria clouds the real issues for Mexico and for the United States. The question is not whether the Mexican state will fail. It will not. The Mexican state does, and will continue to, collect taxes, run schools, repair roads, pay salaries, and manage large social programs throughout the country. The civilian-controlled military has already extinguished any real guerrilla threats. The government regularly holds free and fair elections, and its legitimacy, in the eyes of its citizens and of the world, is not questioned.

The actual risk of the violence today is that it will undermine democracy tomorrow. What has changed in Mexico in recent years is not the drug trade but that a fledgling market-based democracy has arisen. Although an authoritarian legacy persists, power now comes from the ballot box. This transformation has coincided with the rise of Mexico's middle class, which, now nearly 30 million strong, has supported more open politics and markets.

But Mexico's democratic system is still fragile. And by disrupting established payoff systems between drug traffickers and government officials, democratization unwittingly exacerbated drug-related violence. The first two freely elected governments have struggled to respond, hampered by electoral competition and the decentralization of political power. Yet in the long run, only through true democratic governance will Mexico successfully conquer, rather than just paper over, its security challenges. For the safety and prosperity of Mexico and the United States, Washington must go beyond its current focus on border control to a more ambitious goal: supporting Mexico's democracy.

The End of the Government-Controlled Drug Trade

Mexico's escalating violence is in part an unintended side effect of democratization and economic globalization. The chaos, anarchy, and violence of the Mexican Revolution—which began nearly a hundred years ago—scarred the country and enabled the rise of a strong state dominated by a single political party. Created in 1929, the National Revolutionary Party, later renamed the Institutional Revolutionary Party (PRI), systematically extended its control over Mexico's territory and people. It quelled political opposition by incorporating important social groups—including workers, peasants, businesspeople, intellectuals, and the military—into its party structure.

The PRI's reach went beyond politics; it created Mexico's ruling economic and social classes. Through an inwardly focused development model (and later by giving away oil money), the government granted monopolies to private-sector supporters, paid off labor leaders, and doled out thousands of public-sector jobs. It provided plum positions and national recognition for loyal intellectuals, artists, and journalists. Famously called "the perfect dictatorship," the PRI used its great patronage machine (backed, of course, by a strong repressive capacity) to subdue dissident voices—and control Mexico for decades.

Ties between the PRI and illegal traders began in the first half of the twentieth century, during Prohibition. By the end of World War II, the relationship between drug traffickers and the ruling party had solidified. Through the Mexican Ministry of the Interior and the federal police, as well as governorships and other political offices, the government established patron-client relationships with drug traffickers (just as it did with other sectors of the economy and society). This arrangement limited violence against public officials, top traffickers, and civilians; made sure that court investigations never reached the upper ranks of cartels; and defined the rules of the game for traffickers. This compact held even as drug production and transit accelerated in the 1970s and 1980s.

Mexico's political opening in the late 1980s and 1990s disrupted these long-standing dynamics. As the PRI's political monopoly ended, so, too, did its control over the drug trade. Electoral competition nullified the unwritten understandings, requiring drug lords to negotiate with the new political establishment and encouraging rival traffickers to bid for new market opportunities. Accordingly, Mexico's drug-related violence rose first in opposition-led states. After the PRI lost its first governorship, in Baja California in 1989, for example, drug-related violence there surged. In Chihuahua, violence followed an opposition takeover in 1992. When the PRI won back the Chihuahua governorship in 1998, the violence moved to Ciudad Juárez—a city governed by the National Action Party (PAN).

With the election of Vicente Fox, the PAN candidate, as president in 2000, the old model—dependent on PRI dominance—was truly broken. Drug-trafficking organizations took advantage of the political opening to gain autonomy, ending their subordination to the government. They focused instead on buying off or intimidating local authorities in order to ensure the safe transit of their goods.

Democratic competition also hampered the state's capacity to react forcefully. Mexico's powerful presidency—the result of party cohesion rather than institutional design—ended. As Congress' influence grew, legislative gridlock weakened President Fox's hand, delaying judicial and police reforms. Conflicts also emerged between the different levels of government. Federal, state, and local officials—who frequently belonged to different parties—often refused to coordinate policies or even share information. At the extreme, this led to armed standoffs—not with drug dealers but between federal, state, and local police forces, such as the one that occurred in Tijuana in 2005.

Catering Markets to
U.S. Drug Consumption

As democratization tilted the balance of power from politicians to criminals, the economics of Mexico's drug business also changed. Mexico has a long history of supplying coveted but illegal substances to U.S. consumers, beginning at the turn of the twentieth century with heroin and marijuana. It continued through Prohibition, as drinkers moved south and Mexican rumrunners sent alcohol north. The marijuana trade picked up in the 1960s and 1970s with rising demand from the U.S. counterculture. In the late 1970s and 1980s, U.S. cocaine consumption boomed, and Mexican traffickers teamed up with Colombian drug lords to meet the growing U.S. demand.

In the 1980s and 1990s, the United States cracked down on drug transit through the Caribbean and Miami. As a result, more products started going through Mexico and over the U.S.-Mexican border. In 1991, 50 percent of U.S.-bound cocaine came through Mexico; by 2004, 90 percent of U.S.-bound cocaine (and large percentages of other drugs) did. Like other Mexican industries, the drug cartels learned to maximize the comparative advantage of sharing a border with the world's largest consumer. As the transit of drugs to the United States grew, Mexican traffickers gained more power vis-à-vis the Colombian cartels.

These changes in business and enforcement accelerated the consolidation and professionalization of Mexico's drug-trafficking organizations. Rising profitability meant larger operations and more money, and as political and market uncertainty grew, the cartels developed increasingly militarized enforcement arms. The most famous of these branches is the

Zetas, who were recruited from an elite Mexican army unit in the 1990s by the Gulf cartel. This group now acts independently, supplying hired guns and functioning as a trafficking organization itself. For many Mexicans, its name has come to signify terror and bloodshed.

From this increasingly sophisticated operational structure, Mexico's drug-trafficking organizations aggressively moved into the markets for heroin and methamphetamine in the United States, as well as the expanding European cocaine market. They extended their influence down the production chain into source countries such as Bolivia, Colombia, and Peru. They established beachheads in Central American and Caribbean nations—which in many cases have much weaker institutions and democracies than Mexico—where they worked their way into the countries' economic, social, and political fabric, to devastating effect. They widened and deepened their U.S. distribution route. In the words of a recent Justice Department report, Mexican drug cartels now represent the "biggest organized crime threat to the United States," with operations in some 230 U.S. cities. They also diversified their domestic operations, with participants expanding into kidnapping, extortion, contraband, and human smuggling.

Government Response Brings More Bloodshed

The current surge in violence is largely a result of these long-term political and economic processes, but President Calderón's self-proclaimed war on drug trafficking has also contributed. Soon after coming into office in December 2006, Calderón sent the army to Nuevo León, Guerrero, Michoacán, and Tijuana, beginning a new phase of government action that now involves some 45,000 troops. Record numbers of interdictions, arrests, and extraditions to the United States have interrupted business as usual. With the older kingpins gone, the second and often third generations of criminal leaders are now vying for territory, control, and power. Many of these aspiring leaders come from the enforcement arms of the cartels—and are accordingly inclined to use even more violence as they try to gain control of fragmented markets. Both the rewriting and the enforcement of illicit contracts mean blood in the streets. . . .

This history does not diminish the current danger. It does, however, highlight the inefficacy of rehashing past policy approaches. This is not the first time Mexico has brought out the military to quell drug-related violence. President Miguel de la Madrid mobilized troops in the mid-1980s to fight drug gangs, and every subsequent Mexican president has followed suit (although Calderón's current effort far surpasses former shows of force). The United States, too, provided equipment, training, and capacity building at various points throughout the 1980s and 1990s. If history is any lesson, these approaches will neither stem the violence nor provide real border security.

Growing Democracy to Defeat Cartels

Instead, the United States needs to develop a comprehensive policy to bolster North American security—one that treats Mexico as an equal and permanent partner. Mexico must continue to challenge the drug cartels, and the United States, in turn, must address its own role in perpetuating the drug trade and drug-related violence. But more important, Mexico and the United States need to work together to broaden their focus beyond immediate security measures—fostering Mexico's democracy and growing middle class. Only then can they overcome the security challenges facing both nations.

To start, the United States needs to take a hard look at its own role in the escalating violence and instability in Mexico. This means enforcing its own laws—and rethinking its own priorities. When it comes to the gun trade, U.S. law prohibits the sale of weapons to foreign nationals or "straw buyers," who use their clean criminal records to buy arms for others. It also forbids the unlicensed export of guns to Mexico. Nevertheless, over 90 percent of the guns seized in Mexico and traced are found to have come from the United States. These include not just pistols but also cartel favorites such as AR-15s and AK-47-style semiautomatic rifles. To stop this "iron river" of guns, Washington must inspect traffic on the border going south—not just north—and increase the resources for the Bureau of Alcohol, Tobacco, Firearms and Explosives [ATF]. (Even with recent additional deployments, a mere 250 ATF officers and inspectors cover the 2,000-mile border.) This effort should also include a broader program of outreach and education, encouraging responsible sales at gun shops and shows and deterring potential straw buyers with more explicit warnings of the punishment they would face if caught. Reducing the tools of violence in Mexico is a first step in addressing U.S. responsibility.

Even more important than guns, although less discussed, is money. Estimates of illicit profits range widely, but most believe some $15 billion to $25 billion heads across the U.S. border into the hands of Mexico's drug cartels each year. This money buys guns, people, and power. Compiled from thousands of retail drug sales in hundreds of U.S. cities, much of this money is wired, carried, or transported to the U.S.-Mexican border and then simply driven south in bulk. Mexican criminal organizations then launder the funds by using seemingly legal business fronts, such as used-car lots, import-export businesses, or foreign exchange houses. Laundered money not used to fund criminal operations or pay off officials in Mexico is often sent back to the United States and saved in U.S. bank accounts. . . .

Law enforcement, however, is not enough. The supply of drugs follows demand. The United States needs to shift the emphasis of its drug policy toward demand reduction. Studies show that a dollar spent on reducing demand in the United States is vastly more effective than a dollar spent on eradication and interdiction abroad and that money designated for the treatment of addicts is five times as effective as that spent on conventional law enforcement. The United States needs to expand its drug-treatment and drug-education programs and other measures to rehabilitate addicts and lessen drugs' allure for those not yet hooked. Reduced demand would lower the drug profits that corrupt officials, buy guns, and threaten Mexico's democracy.

The United States Needs to Help Mexico

As the United States deals with the problems in its own backyard, it should also be helping Mexico address its challenges. Until just last year [2008], the United States provided less than $40 million a year in security funding to its southern neighbor—in stark contrast to the $600 million designated for Colombia. This changed last June with Congress' passage of the Mérida Initiative, which called for supplying $1.4 billion worth of equipment, software, and technical assistance to Mexico's military, police, and judicial forces over three years.

Despite its many laudable elements, the Mérida Initiative does not go far enough fast enough. For one thing, it is just too small. The current budget for Plan Colombia is twice as large as Mexico's 2009 allotment—and that is for a country that does not share a border with the United States. And even the support for Plan Colombia pales next to the billions of dollars U.S. drug consumers supply to Mexico's enemies in this confrontation. Compared to other U.S. national security threats, Mexico remains an afterthought.

The spending has also been far too slow. Although $700 million had been released by Congress as of April 2009, only $7 million had been spent. Despite the touted urgency, a cumbersome consultation process between the two countries, combined with a complicated disbursement process (since all of the assistance is in kind, not cash), has meant little headway even as the deaths mount. Most important, the focus of this aid is too narrow, reflecting a misunderstanding of Mexico's fundamental challenge. Unlike Colombia, which had to retake vast swaths of territory from guerrilla groups, paramilitary organizations, and drug cartels, the Mexican state has been able to quell the rising violence when it has deployed large and well-armed military units. So far, the cartels have put up limited resistance in the face of true shows of force by the state—for instance, when the government sent in 7,000 troops to Ciudad Juárez in March 2009. Firepower is not the main issue; sustainability is.

Mexico's Achilles' heel is corruption—which in an electoral democracy cannot be stabilizing the way it was in the days of Mexico's autocracy. Under the PRI, the purpose of government policy was to assert power rather than govern by law. The opacity of court proceedings, the notorious graft of the police forces, and the menacing presence of special law enforcement agencies were essential elements of an overall system of political, economic, and social control. Rather than acting as a check or balance on executive power, the judiciary was often just another arm of the party, used to reward supporters and intimidate opponents. Law enforcement, too, was used to control, rather than protect, the population.

The decline of the PRI and the onset of electoral competition transformed the workings of the executive and legislative branches quite quickly, but the changes have had much less influence over the judicial branch or over law enforcement more generally. Instead, even after the transition to democracy, accountability mechanisms remain either nonexistent or defunct. Most of Mexico's various police forces continue to be largely incapable of objective and thorough investigations, having never received adequate resources or training. Impunity reigns: The chance of being prosecuted, much less convicted, of a crime is extremely low. As a result, Mexicans place little faith in their law enforcement and judicial systems. And as today's democratic government struggles to overcome this history through legislative reform, funding new programs for vetting and training and creating more avenues for citizen involvement, it faces a new threat: increasingly sophisticated, well-funded, and autonomous criminal organizations intent on manipulating the rule of law for their own benefit.

The Mérida Initiative provides some funding for institution building, but that is dwarfed by the amount spent on hardware. Furthermore, although Mexico's lawlessness is most intractable at the state and local levels, the Mérida funding focuses almost solely on the federal level. This neglects some 325,000 officers—90 percent of the nation's police. It leaves out those on the front lines who are most likely to face the ultimate Faustian bargain—money or death—from organized crime. The United States should expand Mérida's focus to incorporate local and state-level initiatives and training, including vetting mechanisms similar to those envisioned for federal agents, training for local crime labs, training for judges and lawyers, and support for community policing programs. In the end, all lasting security is local.

Bolstering Mexico's Economic Performance

Improving security will depend above all, however, on other dimensions of the complex U.S.-Mexican relationships—including trade, economic development, and immigration. To really overcome Mexico's security challenges, the United States must move beyond a short-term threat-based mentality to one that considers all these elements in the strategic relationship with its southern neighbor.

The foremost challenge in Mexico today, at least according to most Mexicans, is in fact the growing economic crisis. Even during Mexico's protectionist days, its fortunes rose and fell along with those of its northern neighbor. Today, the economies and general well-being of Mexico and the United States are even more linked. Some 80 percent of Mexico's exports—well over $200 billion worth—go to the United States. Mexico's tourism industry—which brings in $11 billion annually—depends on 15 million American vacationers each year. The large Mexican and Mexican American populations living in the United States—estimated at 12 million and 28 million, respectively—transfer nearly $25 billion a year to family and friends in Mexico.

This relationship runs the other way as well. After Canada, Mexico is the second most important destination for U.S. exports, receiving one-ninth of U.S. goods sent abroad. It is either the primary or the secondary destination for exports from 22 of the 50 U.S. states. Hundreds of thousands—if not millions—of American jobs depend on consumers and industries in Mexico. And increasingly, U.S. citizens depend on Mexico for even more, as over one million individual Americans—from young professionals to adventurous snowbirds—now live there. . . .

In its own self-interest, the United States should work with Mexico on a new economic development strategy. The United States can start by lessening the barriers to trade with Mexico. This will require resolving the current trucking dispute (fulfilling U.S. obligations under the North American Free Trade Agreement [NAFTA] by allowing Mexican trucks to operate on both sides of the border) and avoiding protectionist measures, such as the recent "Buy American" provision in the stimulus package. It will also require investing in the border itself. Nearly one million people and $1 billion in trade cross the border every day, overwhelming the existing infrastructure and border personnel and leading to long and unpredictable border delays, which limit Mexico's competitiveness. The U.S. Department of Transportation currently estimates that $11 billion more will need to be spent on the U.S. side of the border to catch up with the growing traffic.

The United States should also help create opportunities within Mexico. This means expanding development assistance, rather than just security assistance. At less than $5 million for

2009, current U.S. development aid to Mexico is paltry. In-creased assistance should focus on supporting Mexico's efforts to expand its education and infrastructure programs and en-courage local entrepreneurship and job creation.

Intertwined with both the economy and security is immi-gration. Economic opportunities in the United States, and their absence at home, draw millions of Mexicans north. Sub-sequent remittances provide a lifeline for millions of Mexican households and have brought many families out of poverty and into the bottom rungs of Mexico's middle class. At the same time, immigration to the United States pulls away many of Mexico's best and brightest, limiting the spillover benefits of their work on the larger economy and society. . . .

The Importance of Supporting Mexico's Middle Class

U.S. leaders and the press commonly tout President Calderón's commitment to fighting the Mexican cartels as something ex-ceptional. Congressman Connie Mack (R-Fla.) has said, for example, "This is a president who has taken the drug cartels head-on, and has not flinched in the fight to rid Mexico of these cowards." Although true, this image misses the real po-litical dynamic behind Calderón's fight. Rather than a quixotic lone crusader, he is a shrewd politician responding to voter demands.

Like his predecessor, Calderón was elected by Mexico's burgeoning middle class—now nearly one-third of the popu-lation. Long noted for the disparities between the extremely wealthy and the desperately poor, Mexico now has an eco-nomic center that is rapidly expanding. The middle class has grown thanks to NAFTA and Mexico's broader economic opening, a boom in immigration to the United States that has sent billions of dollars back to families at home, and a decade of economic stability and growth that has enabled average citizens to work, save, and plan for the future. Mexico's middle-class families work in small businesses, own their cars and homes, and strive to send their children to college. And as voters, they threw out the PRI in 2000, bringing an end to its 70-year rule. Since then, they have been behind halting steps to create new civil-society organizations and to demand public transparency, judicial reform, and safety. It is these voters who tilted the election in Calderón's favor in 2006—and it is to them he is responding.

Security ranks second only to the economy in terms of voter priorities. Polls show that the middle class (as well as other segments of society) wants the government to take on the narcotraffickers, even if it creates more violence in the short run—and even though many think the government cannot win. Calderón's ratings have risen as he has confronted organized crime, with fully two-thirds of the public supporting his actions.

Mexican middle-class preferences for law and order, fairness, transparency, and democracy benefit Mexico, but they also benefit the United States. Although hardly an antidote for all challenges, a secure and growing middle class would help move Mexico further down the road toward achieving democratic prosperity and toward an increasingly able partnership with the United States. But if this center is diminished or decimated by economic crisis, insecurity, or closing opportunities, Mexico could truly descend into crime-ridden political and economic turmoil.

The best the United States and Mexico can hope for in terms of security is for organized crime in Mexico to become a persistent but manageable law enforcement problem, similar to illegal businesses in the United States. But both the United States and Mexico should hope for more in terms of Mexico's future, and for the future of U.S.-Mexican relations. U.S. policies that help increase accountability, expand economic and social opportunity, and strengthen the rule of law in Mexico will all encourage a more inclusive and more stable democracy there. This will require a difficult conceptual shift in Washington—recognizing Mexico as a permanent strategic partner rather than an often-forgotten neighbor.

| "Mexicans justifiably have long consid-
ered their police suspect. But today
many of those wearing the badge are
even more brazenly bad."

Police Corruption Is Abetting Drug Violence in Mexico

Dudley Althaus

In the following viewpoint, Dudley Althaus, a reporter for the Houston Chronicle, *claims that police corruption in Mexico is rampant. According to Althaus, the Mexican authorities have tried several times to purge corrupt officers from the ranks, but officers are still known to take bribes and abet criminal activity. Unfortunately, crusaders who stand up to drug cartels and other gangs often end up dead, Althaus reports. Though the Mexican government has launched a war against these gangs, the influence and resources of the criminal syndicates have blunted reform efforts, Althaus asserts, leaving many citizens unsure of how law enforcement could ever succeed in eradicating or taming the plague.*

As you read, consider the following questions:

1. About how many federal law enforcement agents does Mexico have, as Althaus reports?

2. According to official estimations quoted by the author, about how much money do drug lords pay in bribes each month to police officers?

3. Which Mexican mayor was found slain after he vowed to clean up the police force in his city?

City cops killing their own mayors; state jailers helping inmates escape; federal agents mutinying against corrupt commanders; outgunned officers cut down in ambushes or assassinated because they work for gangster rivals.

Always precariously frayed, Mexico's thin blue line seems ready to snap.

Six prison guards were killed Wednesday [in October 2010] as they left their night shift in Chihuahua City, 200 miles south of El Paso. On Tuesday, the head of a police commander supposedly investigating the death of an American on the Texas border was packed into a suitcase and sent to a local army base.

Mexicans justifiably have long considered their police suspect. But today many of those wearing the badge are even more brazenly bad: either unwilling or unable to squelch the lawless terror that's claimed nearly 30,000 lives in less than four years.

State and local forces, which employ 90 percent of Mexico's 430,000 officers, find themselves outgunned, overwhelmed and often purchased outright by gangsters.

Paying the Consequences for Corruption

Despite some dramatic improvements—aided by U.S. dollars and training under the $1.6 billion Mérida Initiative [a U.S.-Mexican plan to cooperatively curb drug supply and demand]

—Mexico's 32,000 federal police remain spread thin and hobbled by graft. And many in Mexico consider the American investment little help so far against the bloody tide wrought by drug gangs.

Grasping for a cure, President Felipe Calderón and other officials are pushing to unify Mexico's nearly 2,000 municipal police under 32 state agencies that they insist can better withstand the criminals' volleys of bullets and cash.

"The tentacles of organized crime have touched everyone," said Ignacio Manjarrez, who oversees public security issues for a powerful business association in Chihuahua, the state bordering West Texas that has become Mexico's most violent. "There are some who are loyal to their uniform and others who will take money from anyone and everyone.

"We let it into our society. Now we are paying the consequences."

Purging Police Ranks

Across Mexico, local, state and federal police forces have been purged, then purged again. Veteran officers and recruits alike undergo polygraphs, drug tests and background checks. A national database has been set up to ensure that those flushed from one force don't resurface in another.

Still the plague persists.

One of the surest signals that rivals are going to war over a community or smuggling routes are the dumped corpses of cops who start turning up dead. Many, if not most, of the officers are targeted because they work for one gang or the other.

Scores of federal officers rebelled this summer [of 2010], accusing their commanders of extortion in Ciudad Juarez, the murderous border city that Calderón pledged to pacify. As a result, Mexican officials fired a tenth of the federal police force.

The warden and some guards at a Durango state prison were arrested in July after a policeman confessed in a taped gangland interrogation that they aided an imprisoned crime boss's nightly release so he could kill his enemies.

Another prison warden and scores of guards were detained in August following the breakout of 85 gangsters in Reynosa, on the Rio Grande near McAllen.

On Friday, the governor of Tamaulipas state, which borders South Texas, ordered the purging of the police force in the important port city of Tampico. Gov. Eugenio Hernandez said he took the action following officers' apparent participation in this week's brief abduction of five university students in the city.

Crooked Cops Are Rewarded; Crusaders Are Killed

Mexico's top federal policeman, Genaro García Luna, has estimated gangsters pass out some $100 million each month to local and state cops on the take.

"There really is no internal capacity or appetite to try to get their arms around corruption," said a former U.S. official with intimate knowledge of Mexico's security forces. "Anyone who sticks their head up, wanting to make a change, is eliminated."

Edelmiro Cavazos, mayor of Santiago, a picturesque Monterrey suburb, had vowed after taking office to clean up its police force, which many believe is controlled by the gangster band known as the Zetas.

He barely got the chance to try.

Killers came for him in August, arriving at his home on five trucks, a surveillance tape showing their headlights slicing the night like knives as his own police bodyguard waved them in.

A workman found Cavazos' blindfolded and bound body a few days later, tortured, shot three times and dumped like rubbish along a highway outside Santiago.

The bodyguard and six other officers from Santiago's police force are among those accused in the killing.

"They considered him an obstacle," the Nuevo Leon state attorney general said.

Following Cavazos' slaying and that of 600 others in the Monterrey area this year, Nuevo Leon Gov. Rodrigo Medina proposed bringing municipal police forces under unified state command.

"We have to act as a common front," Medina told reporters. "If we are divided in isolated forces and we have a united organized crime against us and society, we aren't going to be able to articulate the forceful response we need."

Failed Reforms

The tiny western state of Aguascalientes created a unified police command this week. And Calderón won support for the plan Tuesday from 10 newly elected governors.

"Having institutions that enjoy the full confidence of the public can't be put off," Calderón told the new governors. "The single police command is a crucial element in achieving the peace and tranquility that Mexicans deserve."

Although small training programs for state and local forces exist, American dollars by way of the $1.6 billion Mérida Initiative until now have been aimed mostly at Mexico's federal police.

Intelligence gathering and sharing has been enhanced and computer systems upgraded. U.S. and other foreign experts have given extensive training to a third of the federal force, officials say, with another 10,000 Mexican officers attending workshops.

"Beyond the money, the Mérida plan put information and technology at the disposal of the Mexican government," said

Manlio Fabio Beltrones, president of Mexico's senate, whose Institutional Revolutionary Party [PRI] is widely favored to reclaim the presidency in 2012.

Its critics argue that the U.S. aid has failed to curtail the violence, leaving communities and local police forces at the mercy of gangsters.

Javier Aguayo y Camargo, a retired army general who was replaced as Chihuahua City's police chief this month, said no one has "figured out how to make the reforms work."

"The resources of Mérida remain at the federal level," Aguayo y Carmargo said. "We haven't felt any of it. They need to support the states and municipalities."

Gangs Overwhelm Anticorruption Gains

Chihuahua City, capital of the state bordering West Texas, underscores just how quickly the drug wars have overpowered even the best attempts to strengthen local police.

Under a succession of mayors since the late 1990s, the city's police steadily improved. Hiring standards were raised, record keeping improved, arrest and booking processes [were] overhauled. A citizen's oversight committee was set up with significant influence within the department.

Three years ago [2007], the 1,100-officer force became the first in Mexico to be accredited by CALEA [Commission on Accreditation for Law Enforcement Agencies Inc.], a U.S.-based law enforcement association that rigorously evaluates police administrative standards. Only a handful of other Mexican cities have since won accreditation.

Then Mexico's gangland wars arrived in 2008.

The city of 800,000 has been racked this year [2010] by an average of four killings daily, according to a recent study by *El Heraldo*, the leading local newspaper—about 30 times more than a few years ago. It now ranks as Mexico's third most murderous city, behind Ciudad Juarez and Culiacán, capital of the gangster-infested state of Sinaloa, federal officials say.

Why Creating Accountability Mechanisms Has Not Been Forthcoming in Mexico

[Current police] reform efforts have not been more successful because even with an increased emphasis on vetting, they have not sufficiently confronted corruption. Whether by design or by default, reformers (particularly at the local level) have instead prioritized improving selection criteria, education and training and investing in equipment and technology over developing robust accountability mechanisms. As the latter entails confronting organized crime and the rank-and-file police who supplement their salary with daily bribe payments, state and municipal political and police leaders have opted for less threatening reforms. Such a strategy might provide a long-term foundation for tackling corruption, but in the short term, existing reforms have proven to be insufficient to improve police effectiveness. Creating accountability will also require an effective mid-level command structure promoted based on their merits rather than their personnel ties. Although a civil service–type reform is central to the current package of initiatives, it challenges the tradition of clientelism and confronts considerable opposition and implementation hurdles.

Daniel Sabet,
"Police Reform in Mexico: Advances and Persistent Obstacles,"
Woodrow Wilson International Center for Scholars Working Paper,
May 2010. http://wilsoncenter.org.

Scores of city police officers have been fired for suspected corruption. More than two dozen others have been killed, either gunned down in street battles or assassinated by gangsters.

"If with all this equipment and training they are over-whelmed by the criminals, what happens in other places?" said Manjarrez, the businessman who monitors public security matters in Chihuahua. "As prepared as we were, we never saw this tsunami coming."

> "Amid the raging drug war, Mexican of-
> ficials are trying to fix the police
> through a hurried nationwide effort
> that includes better screening and
> training for candidates on a scale never
> tried here before."

Mexico Is Trying to Clean Up Police Corruption

Ken Ellingwood

Ken Ellingwood reports in the following viewpoint how the Mexican government is attempting to oust corrupt police officers and vet new, trustworthy recruits in an effort to sever the ties between law enforcement and drug cartels. After detailing several of the problems police departments face in Mexico, Ellingwood points out strategies the administration has adopted to make law enforcement more reliable. Among these, Ellingwood cites increasing pay, conducting random lie detector tests, and purchasing new equipment to match the well-armed and technologically sophisticated armies of the drug lords. Stationed in Mexico, Ellingwood is a correspondent for the Los Angeles Times *covering issues concerning that country and Central America.*

As you read, consider the following questions:

1. As Ellingwood states, what private information are police veterans and recruits being forced to disclose under the new hiring policy in Mexico?

2. According to the author, who was charged with the kidnapping of customs administrator Francisco Serrano?

3. In San Luis Potosí, what is the new annual salary for police officers, according to the author?

The lie-detector team brought in by Mexico's top cop was supposed to help clean up the country's long-troubled police. There was just one problem: Most of its members themselves didn't pass, and a supervisor was rigging results to make sure others did.

When public safety chief Genaro García Luna found out, he canned the team, all 50 to 60 members.

"He fired everybody," a senior U.S. law enforcement official said.

But the episode shows how difficult it will be for Mexico to reverse a legacy of police corruption that has tainted whole departments, shattered people's faith in law enforcement and compromised one of society's most basic institutions.

Vetting the Police Department

President Felipe Calderón's 3-year-old drug offensive has laid bare the extent to which crime syndicates have infiltrated police agencies at virtually every level. By blurring the line between crime fighters and gangsters, the rampant graft stands as one of the biggest impediments to the Calderón campaign.

Amid the raging drug war, Mexican officials are trying to fix the police through a hurried nationwide effort that includes better screening and training for candidates on a scale never tried here before.

At the heart of the overhaul is a "new police model" that stresses technical sophistication and trustworthiness and that treats police work as a professional career, not a fallback job.

In steps that are groundbreaking for Mexico, cadets and veteran cops are being forced to bare their credit card and bank accounts, submit to polygraph tests and even reveal their family members to screeners to prove they have no shady connections.

Across Mexico, hundreds of state and municipal officers have been purged from their departments and scores more arrested on charges of colluding with drug gangs.

But Mexico has a habit of trading in one corrupt police agency for another, and it will be a long, uphill struggle to create a law enforcement system that can confront crime and gain the trust of ordinary Mexicans. Until then, crooked cops undermine efforts to strengthen the rule of law and defeat drug cartels.

"If you don't have a safe environment to conduct investigations, then it's going to be extremely difficult to capture the narcos," said the U.S. law enforcement official, who was not authorized to speak publicly. "If you have state police that are corrupt and constantly feeding your movements, investigative movements, to the bad guys, you're not going to get anywhere."

Municipal vs. Federal Law Enforcement

Some people fear that the soaring drug violence and mistrust toward police could spark the formation of death squads or vigilante groups. Already there have been suspicions, though no proof, that dozens of killings have been committed by people taking the law into their own hands. More than 13,800 people have been slain since Calderón declared war on the drug cartels, according to unofficial news media tallies.

Although Mexican federal police are in charge of the crackdown against the cartels, it is at the state and municipal levels where law enforcement is most vulnerable, officials and analysts say. Drug gangs exploit hometown ties, dangle bribes and threaten the lives of officers and their relatives to turn police into a kind of fifth column [secret supporters undermining a larger group from within].

Poorly paid state and municipal officers are often on the payroll of drug smugglers, passing tips, providing muscle or looking the other way when illegal drugs are shipped through their turf.

Criminal infiltration of local departments has worsened as the Mexican political system becomes less centralized and as narcotics traffickers delve into offshoot enterprises, such as kidnapping, theft and extortion, that under Mexican law fall within the jurisdiction of state authorities.

At times, local police have faced off in tense showdowns against Mexican federal police and soldiers. The mistrust often prompts federal authorities to keep their state and municipal counterparts in the dark, aggravating interagency frictions.

"There is a *disorganized* police fighting against *organized* crime," said Guillermo Zepeda, a police expert at the Center of Research for Development [CIDAC] in Mexico City.

In the western state of Michoacán, 10 municipal officers were arrested in the slayings of 12 federal agents there in July [2009]. In the Gulf of Mexico port city of Veracruz, authorities investigating the June disappearance of customs administrator Francisco Serrano detained nearly 50 municipal officers. The then chief of municipal police for the seaport and three traffic officers were later charged with his kidnapping. Serrano is still missing.

The profound flaws of Mexico's police, who are frequently ill trained, poorly equipped and unhappy in their work, are the most visible emblems of how the drug offensive is straining the nation's broader system of law and order.

An opaque and creaky court system groans under the weight of thousands of new drug war cases, and a number of prosecutors, defense lawyers and judges have been slain. Meanwhile, prison officials scramble to make room for the surge of detainees, many of them violent.

The President's Plan to Revamp Police Forces

Calderón's administration has laid out a strategy to expand and revamp the federal police and to force states, cities and towns to modernize and clean up their forces through such tools as polygraphs and drug tests. Standing in the way are many years of graft, turf jealousies, budget constraints and a drug underworld that has greeted every government move with greater viciousness.

García Luna, the public safety chief, has seized the moment to hire thousands of federal cadets, who under the strict new standards must hold at least a university degree. Despite the stiff requirements, the federal force has grown to 32,264 officers, from about 25,000 a year ago.

At a sleek federal campus here in the north-central state of San Luis Potosí, Mexican officials are rushing to turn 9,000 college graduates into federal investigators. The school boasts state-of-the-art lecture halls, computer rooms, workout facilities, a driver-training track and shooting range.

The U.S. government supports the push to expand and professionalize Mexico's federal forces, lending dozens of police instructors as part of a $1.4-billion aid package for Mexico known as the Mérida Initiative.

Federal cadets, dressed in white polo shirts and smart blue jeans, study criminal procedure, interview techniques, criminology and intelligence. The school has graduated 2,234 investigators since June; more than 1,000 fresh recruits began the six-week course last month.

An even more daunting challenge waits in states and cities, which are home to the vast majority of police in Mexico—more than 370,000 officers. In the last two years, the federal government has relied on budget incentives to prod local departments to vet officer candidates and boost salaries, now often as low as $90 a week.

García Luna has gone so far as to call for eliminating the country's 2,022 municipal agencies, widely seen as the weakest link in Mexican law enforcement, and folding them into police departments of the 31 states and Mexico City, which is formally a federal district.

The proposal is controversial, probably requiring a change in the Mexican Constitution and facing opposition from municipal officials from across the political spectrum who are reluctant to yield parts of their fiefdoms.

Some analysts warn that such a plan could make it easier for criminal groups to bribe police.

"Concentrating power at the state level runs the risk of creating a more hierarchical, 'one-stop-shopping' system of high-level corruption," said David Shirk, a University of San Diego professor and a fellow at the Woodrow Wilson Center in Washington.

States and municipalities have moved inconsistently to clean up their forces. In some places, such as the northern city of Chihuahua, police are gradually adopting U.S.-style law enforcement standards, such as those promoted by the private Commission on Accreditation for Law Enforcement Agencies, Inc.

Many analysts are encouraged to see local agencies spending more to improve training, equipment and wages, but see scant improvement on corruption.

"You can train police all day long, but if they're still corrupt, then it doesn't really help," said Daniel Sabet, who teaches at Georgetown University and studies Mexican law enforcement. "The corruption and organized-crime infiltration has not changed."

Building a Better Police Force

Here in San Luis Potosí state, whose police operation is praised by the U.S. as among a handful in Mexico that are sound, officials raised minimum pay to about $700 a month and now offer bonuses of nearly two months' pay to officers who perform well and pass twice-yearly vetting.

Cesareo Carvajal, public safety director until the state government changed hands in September, said he fired about 150 of 3,000 officers during his two-year term.

The agency also bought radio equipment, new weaponry and police vehicles, and outfitted officers with redesigned uniforms to create an updated image.

At a state-run police academy where San Luis Potosí's next generation of police is being molded, the rhythmic *thump-thump* of boots on pavement echoed on a recent morning as officers-in-training practiced marching.

Cadets here say a new, trustworthy breed of Mexican police is possible—but that it will take time to build.

As part of a stricter selection process, recruit Hiram Viñas was hooked to a lie detector and asked about any past scrapes with the law. Screeners peeked into his bank account and rummaged in his family's background.

Viñas, 24, wearing a blue windbreaker and buzz cut, said the rigorous scrutiny could help win over Mexican society.

"They are applying tests and evaluations now that had never been done in our country," he said. "I think over time, people will learn to trust the police again."

> *"Fifteen years [after the passage of NAFTA], Mexico is still unable to create enough jobs to employ its people. Out-migration has doubled, and on both sides of the US-Mexico border labor-market competition has kept wages down."*

NAFTA Has Contributed to Economic and Governmental Instability in Mexico

Jeff Faux

According to Jeff Faux, the North American Free Trade Agreement (NAFTA)—brokered among Canada, the United States, and Mexico—was designed, in part, to raise the value of Mexican imports and reduce joblessness in that country. Instead, Faux reports in the following viewpoint, cheaper Chinese exports undercut Mexico's exports, leaving the promises of NAFTA unfulfilled. Faux also contends that because NAFTA opened Mexican businesses and banks to foreign investment and ownership, profits from these organizations are not being recycled back into Mexican society but are invested elsewhere around the globe. Finally, Faux claims the trade agreement has abetted the drug

Jeff Faux, "So Far from God, so Close to Wall St." *Nation*, vol. 289, August 3, 2009, pp. 15–18. Copyright © 2009 by The Nation (New York). Reproduced by permission.

trade by expanding trade routes between Mexico and America, creating new recruits from the multitude of Mexican farmers who became unemployed after finding they could not compete against the American agricultural industry, and providing Mexican drug lords with US weaponry that they can use to fight their private wars. Faux believes President Barack Obama should seize the opportunity to renegotiate NAFTA so that it works for citizens of all three trade partners instead of just the elite investors looking for quick money. Faux is the founder of the Economic Policy Institute, a liberal think tank advocating global economic justice, and the author of The Global Class War: How America's Bipartisan Elite Lost Our Future—and What It Will Take to Win It Back.

As you read, consider the following questions:

1. According to Faux, what percentage of the Mexican banking system is owned by foreign investors?

2. As the author reports, in the 1990s, the Mexican drug cartels successfully outmuscled what other country's suppliers to take over the selling of cocaine to US markets?

3. As Faux states, what percentage of Mexicans lives on less than $2 per day?

This past winter [of 2008/2009] both the outgoing director of the CIA [Michael Hayden] and a separate Pentagon report declared political instability in Mexico to be on a par with Pakistan and Iran as top-ranking threats to US national security. It was an exaggeration; Mexico is not yet a "failed state." On the other hand, it is certainly drifting in that direction.

A vicious war among narco-trafficking cartels last year killed at least 6,000 people, including public officials, police and journalists. The country leads the world in kidnappings

(Pakistan is second). And with the global crisis, the chronically anemic economy is hemorrhaging jobs, businesses and hope.

Not surprisingly, voters turned against President Felipe Calderón's right-wing National Action Party (PAN) in the July 5 midterm elections. But the left-wing Democratic Revolutionary Party (PRD)—which many believe was robbed of the presidency in the 2006 election—has ripped itself apart with factional infighting. So frustrated Mexicans gave their Congress back to the Institutional Revolutionary Party (PRI), whose decades of corrupt authoritarian rule were supposed to have permanently ended in 2000. At least, thought many voters, the PRI knows how to keep order.

Mexicans are of course responsible for their own country. But geography has always forced them to play out their history in the shadow of their northern neighbor. "Poor Mexico," goes the saying. "So far from God, so close to the United States." Today, Mexico is a prime example of the socially destructive effects of the neoliberal economics promoted throughout the world by the US governing class.

NAFTA's Failed Promises

The North American Free Trade Agreement [NAFTA]—proposed by Ronald Reagan, negotiated by George Bush I and pushed through Congress by Bill Clinton in 1993—is both symbol and substance of neoliberalism. It was sold to the citizens of the United States, Mexico and Canada with the promise that free trade in goods and money would transform Mexico into a booming middle-class economy, dramatically reducing illegal immigration and creating a vast market for US and, to a lesser extent, Canadian exports.

Fifteen years later, Mexico is still unable to create enough jobs to employ its people. Out-migration has doubled, and on both sides of the US-Mexico border labor-market competition has kept wages down. At the top, income and wealth have ballooned. It is no accident that among NAFTA's prominent god-fathers were former Treasury Secretary Robert Rubin (Democrat) and former Federal Reserve chair Alan Greenspan (Republican), whose fingerprints are all over the current global financial disaster.

I was an opponent of NAFTA. Still, I thought the best case for it was that efficiencies from economic integration could at least make US and Mexican businesses more internationally competitive. But even that argument turned out to be worth no more than a share of [investment con artist] Bernie Madoff's hedge fund.

Several years ago I gave a speech to a group of business-people in Mexico City. Those from the multinational banks and corporations thought NAFTA was a great success, but smaller Mexican businessmen saw it differently. You Americans, said one, promised that with your technology and our cheap labor, we'd be partners in competing with Asia. Then you opened up your markets to China and invested there instead. "Sure," he said. "We can make TV parts for half what it costs in the United States. But the Chinese can make them, and ship them, for a tenth. So instead of closing the gap between Mexico and the United States by raising wages, we have to narrow the gap between Mexico and China by lowering them."

When I mentioned the conversation to a New York investment banker who had lobbied for NAFTA, he conceded that his side may have talked vaguely about partnership with Mexico. But he shrugged and added, "Things changed"—that is, profit opportunities in China dwarfed anything Mexico had to offer.

Investing Mexican Money Elsewhere

The Wall Streeters had little interest in making Mexico more competitive. They also had little interest in making the United States more competitive. Their purpose was just the opposite:

to disconnect themselves and their corporate partners from the fate of any particular country. The World Trade Organization, the opening of the US market to China and a parade of bilateral trade agreements followed in NAFTA's wake.

In Mexico, the political and financial elite were willing collaborators. For example, NAFTA opened up Mexican banks to foreign ownership: Political insiders who had bought the giant Banamex from the government for $3.2 billion and gotten the government to provide it with permanent subsidies then sold the firm, with the subsidies, to Citigroup for $12.5 billion. Today roughly 90 percent of the banking system is owned by US and other foreign investors, who do not have to recycle Mexicans' deposits, or the Mexican government's money, back into Mexico but can invest them anyplace in the world.

The Banamex deal was negotiated by Rubin after he became Citigroup's $17 million-a-year executive committee chair. In the late 1980s, when he was at Goldman Sachs, Rubin had midwifed the privatization of Mexico's phone system to Carlos Slim, a politically connected Mexican businessman. Slim then used the monopoly profits from his high phone rates to invest all over the globe—including a substantial ownership stake in the *New York Times*. The latest *Forbes* rating says he's the world's third-richest man.

Still, as long as the US economy was blowing dot-com and subprime bubbles, the neoliberal model seemed stable. US investors got Mexican bank deposits and cheaper labor on both sides of the border. Through out-migration to the States, Mexico's oligarchs [government by the few] got rid of frustrated workers who might otherwise have been politically troublesome. The economy also benefited from hard-currency remittances migrants sent back home.

Benefiting the Drug Trade

Another infusion of cash to the Mexican economy, unacknowledged in the official statistics, is the roughly $25 billion in illegal drug exports to the States. Today, with remittances, oil prices and tourism depressed, the narco trade is probably Mexico's largest single earner of hard currency.

NAFTA and the neoliberal ideology it represents are certainly not the root causes of narco-trafficking. But they have been major factors in its recent monstrous growth. For starters, the trade agreement created a two-way overland superhighway for contraband; the Mexican drug lords use the dollars they have earned from their exports to import guns, aircraft and sophisticated military equipment from the United States to fight their territorial wars. By wiping out small Mexican farms that could not compete with heavily subsidized US agribusiness, NAFTA also expanded the pool of unemployed young people that provides the narco-traffickers with recruits. And banking integration under NAFTA made money laundering much easier.

Perhaps most important, NAFTA has helped maintain the corrupt network of Mexican oligarchs. The 1988 presidential election—which the then ruling PRI had to steal from the PRD to win—shocked the establishment on both sides of the border. By opening up Mexico to US money and influence, NAFTA was a way, as the US Trade Representative said to me at the time, "to keep the Mexican left out of power."

Until the 1980s, Mexican drug (mostly marijuana) smuggling to the north was modest in scale and generally tolerated by successive PRI governments. Their message was: We don't care what you sell to the gringos, but no rough stuff here, keep it away from our kids and of course share a little of the profit under the table. But the US-backed neoliberals who took over the PRI in the 1980s had closer ties with the Mexican cartels. The brother and father of president and NAFTA champion Carlos Salinas—hailed in Washington as a good-government reformer—were widely accused of being connected to the drug business. In Salinas's first year in office his national police chief was found with $2.4 million in drug money in the trunk of his car.

In the 1990s, as the geographically better-positioned Mexican cartels muscled out the Colombians as chief cocaine retailers to the US market, their profits and political influence grew. But so did the rivalry among them and their allied government factions for control of trade routes. Bullet-riddled bodies began showing up on the streets, making the public nervous.

Seeking legitimacy after his 2006 election was tainted by charges of fraud, President Felipe Calderón declared war on the narco-traffickers. It was a popular gesture, but given that the police, the military and the legal system are heavily infiltrated by the gangs, it backfired. The narcos reacted with horrific violence—assassinations, beheadings and mutilations of police and soldiers as well as thugs, brazenly displayed on YouTube. Losing control, Calderón appealed to George Bush II for help. The result: the Mérida Initiative, a $400 million-per-year program to provide aircraft, military equipment and training to the Mexican police and military.

Rethinking NAFTA After the Global Financial Crisis

After decades of keeping its distance from the United States, the Mexican military—like the armed forces of Colombia, Honduras and other Latin American countries—is becoming a Pentagon client. In turn, Mexican society is itself becoming militarized. Corrupt local police are being replaced by soldiers who may be slightly less corrupt but who are a greater threat to human rights and democracy. An April Human Rights Watch report identified seventeen specific cases of abuse by the Mexican military, including "killings, torture, rapes, and arbitrary detentions."

To his credit, Barack Obama has acknowledged what his predecessors failed to: that the US demand for drugs and its supplying of arms makes it an enabler in the rise of narco warlords. But he has also made it clear that neither issue is on his administration's agenda. Moreover, just as Bill Clinton carried the water for George Bush I's NAFTA, Barack Obama has endorsed Bush II's [George W. Bush] Mérida Initiative.

Given the unwillingness of US politicians to deal with the demand side of the market, the Mérida Initiative is not likely to be any more successful in eradicating the drug trade than the $6 billion Plan Colombia has been. The best one can hope for is some sort of market-sharing deal among the cartels that would be implicitly endorsed by the Mexican government while Washington tactfully averts its eyes. Given that in many areas, drug money is the chief source of campaign financing, a PRI-dominated Mexican Congress might be just the right forum for a cynical, but welcome, end to the killings.

Meanwhile, the drug violence has frightened away tourists and investors, making Mexico's recession even worse. Most forecasters expect the economy to contract some 6 percent this year [2009]—a huge hit to a country in which 45 percent live on $2 a day or less. Calderón's response is to tread water—rescuing big businesses that speculated on Wall Street derivatives and dribbling out a bit more public spending—while waiting for the United States to once again suck up Mexico's surplus labor.

But even when the US economy recovers, it is unlikely to re-create the credit boom that kept the NAFTA deal afloat. In the post-crash era, the United States will finally be forced to address its trade deficits and its massive foreign debt. Americans will have to slow down consumer spending, increase savings and sell more to—and buy less from—the rest of the world. If Mexico could not prosper during fifteen years of exporting goods and people to a bloated US consumer market, it is hard to believe it will be able to do so when that market has slimmed down.

The entire relationship must be rethought. In this regard, Obama's abandonment of his campaign pledge to renegotiate NAFTA was a missed opportunity. A renewed debate over the trade deal could have spurred public discussion of the failure of neoliberal economics, the "war on drugs" and an immigration policy that ignores conditions in Mexico that drive people across the border. It could have been a forum to think through the question of how continental integration can work for working people rather than just investors. For example, what kind of cooperative transportation, energy and green industrial policies would make the people of three nations—now bound together in one market—globally competitive?

Obama's Wall Street advisers have no more interest in this sort of change than did Bush's. And without a new economic direction, life for the average Mexican will surely worsen and social tensions rise. Some Mexican friends point out that the revolution against Spain erupted in 1810 and the one against the US-backed dictator Porfirio Díaz in 1910. And in 2010. . .?

In any event, Mexico's growing troubles will not stay conveniently on the other side of the Rio Grande. Build a tenfoot wall, and desperate people will find twelve-foot ladders. Free trade will, of course, continue to flourish; Homeland Security Secretary Janet Napolitano estimates that Mexican drug cartels are now operating in 230 US cities.

So, thanks to the people who brought you the subprime mortgage disaster, the credit freeze and the Great Recession, the next Mexican revolution may come closer to home than you think.

Periodical Bibliography

The following articles have been selected to supplement the diverse views presented in this chapter.

Robert C. Bonner "The New Cocaine Cowboys," *Foreign Affairs*, July/August 2010.

Kathleen Bruhn "Mexico: Democracy and the Future," *Insights on Law & Society*, Spring 2009.

Alfredo Corchado "A Fighting Chance," *Wilson Quarterly*, Spring 2009.

Economist "Under the Volcano," October 14, 2010.

Jeff Faux "Obama's Mexican Challenge," *Dissent*, Spring 2009.

William Finnegan "In the Name of the Law," *New Yorker*, October 18, 2010.

Enrique Krauze "The Mexican Evolution," *New York Times*, March 24, 2009.

Guy Lawson "The Making of a Narco State," *Rolling Stone*, March 19, 2009.

David Luhnow "To Root Out Dirty Police, Mexico Sends in a General," *Wall Street Journal*, December 23, 2010.

Michael Petrou "Mexico's Civil War," *Maclean's*, December 8, 2008.

Sam Quinones "State of War," *Foreign Policy*, March/April 2009.

CHAPTER 2

What Has Been the Impact of NAFTA on Mexico?

Chapter Preface

The North American Free Trade Agreement (NAFTA) is an economic pact between the governments of the United States, Canada, and Mexico. Signed into effect in 1994, the agreement eliminated barriers (such as tariffs) between the countries to facilitate trade and encourage foreign investment. While most duties between Canada and the United States had been lifted through prior trade agreements, much of the interest in NAFTA focused on how the easing of restrictions would affect Mexico's economy and on the privileged status that country acquired in US markets. After more than sixteen years in operation, NAFTA has garnered both criticism and praise for its impact on Mexico's agricultural and industrial sectors.

Critics have charged NAFTA with destroying Mexico's agricultural base by opening the doors to cheap US corn that undercut Mexican farmers' prices, pushing many out of business. Some economists have also contended that the agreement has not stimulated Mexican industry but instead has only benefited the maquiladoras, Mexican assembly plants that receive pieces of US products and turn them into finished products that are shipped back to the United States for distribution. Some observers have likened the maquiladora system to sweatshop labor, with shanty towns growing up around US-owned factories that spew pollution into the air and waterways. Writing for *Rolling Stone* on October 28, 1993, William Greider warned, "Anyone who has seen the rank pollution, labor exploitation and industrial slums of the maquiladoras understands why environmentalists, American labor unions and human-rights activists oppose NAFTA." Greider's assertion has been reiterated by numerous critics since NAFTA's passage.

NAFTA's supporters, however, cite statistics that show a growth in Mexican markets—especially in areas such as garment manufacturing, glass and pottery making, and jewelry creation. In a June 16, 2008, report for the National Center for Policy Analysis, Heidi Sommer pointed out that even the controversial maquiladoras have found work for 840,000 Mexicans and that wages for laborers have risen every year since 1994. Daniel Griswold, the associate director of the Center for Trade Policy Studies at the Cato Institute, wrote in a January 8, 2004, opinion piece for Cato that Mexico's economy was progressing and transforming under NAFTA. He asserted:

> Since 1993, the year before the pact took effect, two-way commerce between the United States and Mexico roughly tripled, from $81 billion to $232 billion. . . . NAFTA has helped speed Mexico's dramatic economic and political transformation. The trade agreement marks a major milestone in Mexico's turn away from a closed, centrally directed economic system under the authority of a one-party state, to an open and dynamic market democracy.

Making the change to an open market democracy, however, will require the Mexican government to continue to institute reforms that free it from corruption and other economic stumbling blocks.

Whether observers are optimistic or pessimistic about the impact of NAFTA on Mexico, a few facts reveal a country still struggling to get ahead. Mexico's unemployment rate has increased by 50 percent since late 2007 (to about 5 percent of the population), according to the Organisation for Economic Co-operation and Development. The nation's gross domestic product (GDP) has climbed by only about 2–3 percent each year during that time, and that is quite a bit lower than the GDP growth of the United States and Canada. Though Mexico's exports have been growing, about 90 percent of its trade goes to its NAFTA partners (more than 88 percent to the United States alone). Many experts believe Mexico has to tap other international markets to achieve significant economic growth.

In the chapter that follows, analysts debate the impact NAFTA has had on Mexico's economy. Some argue that the trade agreement has crippled Mexico's productivity; others insist that NAFTA will, in the long term, bring the country great rewards once the government makes good on internal reforms and the global economy weathers the recent financial crisis.

> "More than 15 years after NAFTA, the task for Mexico is to take full advantage of the trade agreement—and to go beyond it."

Mexico Should Capitalize on the Benefits of NAFTA

The Economist

The Economist *is a British newsmagazine that forgoes bylines so that the entire publication speaks with a unified voice. The following viewpoint is an article the* Economist *contributed to the Minneapolis-St.* Paul Star Tribune. *In it, the* Economist *argues that despite negative public opinion about the state of the Mexican economy, export trade with the United States is growing. The* Economist *claims that the North American Free Trade Agreement (NAFTA), which exempts Mexico from US tariff duties, has increased cross-border trade and helped Mexico recover somewhat during the global financial crisis. The* Economist *warns, however, that Mexico has to improve its domestic economic policy to truly take advantage of the gains afforded by NAFTA.*

As you read, consider the following questions:

1. As the *Economist* describes it, what is the "Interpuerto"?

2. According to the author, what is the percentage of Mexico's share of US markets, as of the writing of this viewpoint?

3. Why do some high-tech businesses prefer to negotiate contracts with Mexico over China, according to the *Economist*?

At the moment it is just a thousand acres of mud on the outskirts of Monterrey, a bustling industrial city in northern Mexico. Soon it should be the "Interpuerto," a customs-clearing zone to speed goods on their way to the United States via two rail lines and the highways to which it will be connected.

The aim of the $2 billion project, backed by the state government of Nuevo León and private investors, is to allow cargo to skip the long lines at customs posts on the border 150 miles to the north.

Projects like the Interpuerto matter for Mexico, the economy of which depends on exporting labor-intensive manufactured goods to its giant neighbor. Despite the ratifying of the North American Free Trade Agreement (NAFTA) in 1993, within a decade Mexico's exports to the United States were overtaken by those of China.

The financial crisis and recession north of the border was an even bigger blow: A slump in exports (down by a quarter in the first half of 2009, compared with the same period the previous year) helped to push Mexico's economy into deep recession. Recovery is now under way. But Mexicans remain gloomy about their economic prospects, according to opinion polls. And Mexican businesses worry about the world currency "war": The peso is appreciating against the dollar and, recently, against the yuan, thanks to capital inflows.

Mexico's Resilient Markets

Yet Mexico's trade picture is brighter than it looks. Last year [2009] was less bad for Mexico than for most of the rest of the world. Although its exports shrank, they have recovered quickly. Mexico's share of the U.S. market has grown to 12.2 percent—its highest level since NAFTA came into force. The rapacious expansion of China's exports has come at the expense of others, including Canada, the third NAFTA member.

This resilience reflects various built-in advantages. Geographical proximity has become more valuable as the price of oil (and thus transport) has risen. NAFTA exempts Mexico from the American import tariffs that clobber Chinese exporters. Chinese tiles and paving stones, for instance, are cheaper than Mexican ones, averaging $5.20 per square yard against $5.29, but after paying an 8.5 percent tariff they end up more expensive. The same is true of cloth, glassware, chemicals and much else. The NAFTA effect is also concentrating the manufacture of smaller cars in Mexico. The country's car exports are booming as never before, up 10.5 percent on their level of 2008. Carmakers have announced investment of $4.4 billion over the next four years, according to the government.

Sadly, personal security has become a worry in northern Mexico because of the wave of drug-related violence. But high-tech businesses reckon that their intellectual property is safer there than in China, says Othon Ruiz, Nuevo León's development minister. Partly as a result, consumer-electronics manufacturers have stepped up investment in Mexico in recent years.

Mexico's Domestic Economy Is Sluggish

Even if Mexico continues to gain market share north of the border, the benefit will be limited by the prospect of years of lackluster growth in the U.S. economy. So it is all the costlier that Mexico is not making the most of its advantages. Take the Interpuerto. It does not yet have American permission to stage customs clearance. The easiest way would be to let U.S. officials do checks on Mexican soil, but this raises nationalist hackles among Mexican politicians. (Similarly, the U.S. Congress, in violation of NAFTA, thwarted a pilot scheme under which Mexican long-haul trackers operated north of the border.)

The bigger problem is that a lack of dynamism in the domestic economy caps the gains from trade.

More than 15 years after NAFTA, the task for Mexico is to take full advantage of the trade agreement—and to go beyond it. A sickly American economy may at last provide a powerful incentive to do so.

> "Income disparities in member countries have continued to grow since NAFTA came into effect, most strongly in Mexico."

NAFTA Hurts the Mexican Economy

Anne Vigna

In the following viewpoint, Anne Vigna, a French news correspondent in Mexico, claims that the North American Free Trade Agreement (NAFTA) has hurt the Mexican economy. Vigna asserts that opening up agricultural trade between the United States and Mexico has depressed the value of Mexican crops (especially corn) by flooding the market with cheaper American exports. Vigna maintains that the only winners in Mexico were the maquiladoras, factories that import US components, assemble them, and ship completed products back to the United States. Even these businesses, however, suffered high unemployment when the global economic crisis hit in 2008, she writes. She also warns of looming discussions about the Security and Prosperity Partnership of North America (SPP), a plan to facilitate trade among Mexico, Canada, and the United States. Vigna's fears were never realized as the SPP summits never generated any new policies.

As you read, consider the following questions:

1. According to Vigna, what has happened to the import rate of grain in Mexico since 1994, the year NAFTA took effect?

2. How has the maquiladora system weakened Mexico's economy, in the author's view?

3. What happened to Mexican emigration rates after the passage of NAFTA?

At midnight Jan. 1 [2008], thousands of Mexican farmers formed a human chain at the Ciudad Juárez border crossing into the United States, under an enormous banner with the slogan *Sin maiz no hay pais* ("Without corn there is no country"). It was the 14th anniversary of the North American Free Trade Agreement [NAFTA] linking Canada, Mexico and the U.S.

The farmers were protesting the introduction of complete trade liberalization at the beginning of this year, which means that corn, beans, sugar and powdered milk—the basic foods of Mexico—are no longer subject to import duty.

In some towns, there have been calls for NAFTA to be re-negotiated. Farmers' organizations insist that the consequences of the agreement are beyond dispute.

The U.S. academic Laura Carlsen cited statistics: "Every hour, Mexico imports $1.5 million worth of food. In that same one-hour period, 30 farmers emigrate to the U.S." Opening borders could hurt almost 1.5 million small Mexican farmers.

The only result of competition in agricultural products has been to aggravate already dramatic inequalities among the three countries.

Corn Crisis

Legally, NAFTA's agricultural provisions could be renegotiated, but that isn't on the agenda. In January 2007, Mexico refused to support a Canadian complaint to the World Trade Organization about subsidies to U.S. corn producers.

It is just over a year since the tortilla crisis revived controversy about Mexican dependence on U.S. corn.

The use of corn in the United States to produce ethanol has driven up its price and reduced supplies for food. Since NAFTA came into force, Mexico has become dependent upon subsidized (and therefore cheaper) U.S. corn, and huge imports have ruined Mexican farmers.

Meanwhile, every hike in the price of tortillas threatens millions of Mexicans with hunger. This is why mass protests by women beating saucepans in Mexico City at the beginning of last year forced the government to bring in an extra 600,000 tonnes of white corn from the United States to create an emergency fund and set a price cap.

Mexico has tripled its imports of grain since 1994 and now depends on them for 40 percent of its food needs. "Today Mexico has to rely on imports for basic foodstuffs, whatever the market price," said Armando Bartra, director of the Institute for Rural Development Studies.

An unexpected consequence of the invasion of Mexico by basic and processed U.S. foods is a dramatic increase in obesity. Almost 33 percent of adults are obese; another 40 percent are overweight. The side effects absorb 21 percent of the public health budget.

Mexican President Felipe Calderón tried to deny this in his last New Year's address: "NAFTA has benefited you and me, the consumer, by offering us greater choice and quality at a better price." Even the World Bank recognizes that there is an agricultural crisis.

Sacrificing Mexico's Agricultural Sector

Mexico has effectively admitted to having sacrificed its agricultural sector during negotiations—a criminal failure, given that a third of the population lived from the land in 1994.

Although clauses were included to safeguard vulnerable products for 14 years, these were never invoked. From 1996, Mexico unilaterally decided to allow in vast quantities of U.S. corn, in excess of authorized quotas and duty free. There was a further failure to observe the agreement in 2001, when President Vicente Fox (former head of Coca-Cola for Latin America) allowed the drinks industry to import fructose manufactured from transgenic U.S. corn, rather than supporting Mexico's struggling sugar cane industry.

The U.S. imposed embargos on Mexican products in violation of the agreement and its own laws. Tomato growers from the Pacific state of Sinaloa had to fight for four years to obtain authorization to export their produce to the U.S., which claimed that it was protecting its own farmers in Florida. Now avocado growers in another Pacific state, Michoacán, are struggling against quarantine regulations introduced solely to limit competition.

The Mexican government has terminated most of its rural assistance schemes. According to the Organisation for Economic Co-operation and Development, support for producers fell from 28 percent of gross farm receipts in 1991–93 to 14 percent in 2004–06, and mainly benefited the biggest landholders. At the same time, the U.S. was increasing its support—particularly export subsidies.

Those Who Benefit from NAFTA

According to a paper by researchers at Tufts University's Global Development and Environment Institute, "In environmental terms Mexico's loss is not the United States' gain. The rise in U.S. corn production has provided a stimulus to some of the most environmentally destructive agricultural practices in

Mexican Job Growth Stalls Under NAFTA

It is striking that NAFTA could bring Mexico such large increases in trade and foreign investment but generate so few jobs. Overall, limited employment gains in manufacturing and services have been offset by large employment losses in agriculture. With roughly one million Mexicans entering the labor force each year, the NAFTA model has failed to deliver what Mexico needs the most.

Eduardo Zepeda, Timothy A. Wise, and Kevin P. Gallagher, "Rethinking Trade Policy for Development: Lessons from Mexico Under NAFTA," Carnegie Endowment for International Peace Policy Outlook, December 2009.

the United States. Corn is very chemical-intensive, both in terms of fertilizers and pesticides. Recent expansions of corn production have taken place in some of the drier states, necessitating irrigation at unsustainable levels."

The Mexican government responded to criticism by pointing out that between 1994 and 2007, corn production rose from 18.2 million tonnes to 23.7 million.

There are some winners from NAFTA: the huge farms in the north of Mexico, often owned by U.S. companies, where agricultural laborers work in dreadful conditions. Between 1995 and 2005, the gross domestic product of Mexico's farming sector grew by 1.9 percent per annum, well below that of most South American countries and of its Central American neighbors.

Mexico's economic ministry has tried to put this in perspective, claiming that agricultural statistics do not give a complete picture of trade relations with the U.S.

"We have more to gain by pursuing integration with North America," said James Salazar Salinas, deputy director of the ministry's trade negotiations service. "Non-agricultural sectors have become more important to our economy. Overall, the results of NAFTA have been very positive." NAFTA's defenders insist that it has achieved its purpose of significantly increasing trade between the partners.

Bilateral trade between Mexico and the U.S. has increased by an annual average of more than 10 percent. Mexico is now the U.S.'s third-largest trading partner and the second-largest market for its goods. Trade with Canada has more than doubled, although its overall volume remains modest.

The agreement also led to a significant increase in foreign direct investment. Between 1994 and 2006, U.S. business invested $120 billion in Mexico, more than 60 percent of all investment in the country.

Declining Employment

Increasing trade has not bolstered employment: On average, only 80,000 jobs are created every year for the 730,000 Mexicans who enter the labor market. These are mainly in maquiladoras—factories that assemble components imported from the United States into products for export back to the United States.

"The traditional liberal theory that opening up trade creates employment opportunities in countries with a large workforce is completely wrong," said Sandra Polaski of the Carnegie Endowment for International Peace.

The duty-free import of components has quickly and significantly reduced the indirect effects that this sector might have been expected to have upon the economy and upon employment in particular.

"The maquiladoras currently import 97 percent of their materials," Polaski said. "This trend is being copied in the traditional industrial sector, where production mainly depends upon importing components that, until 1994, were supplied by Mexican manufacturers."

The maquiladora system has weakened Mexico's economy, forcing it to reduce social spending and trying to increase its oil revenues in an attempt to balance its budget.

"Imports of high-value-added products have created a deficit in our trade balance with the U.S.," said Enrique Peter Dussell of the University of Mexico. "This is despite a spectacular increase in the volume of exports."

Since 2001, expansion of the maquiladoras has slowed, which NAFTA's defenders attribute to the effects of 9-11 [referring to the September 11, 2001, terrorist attacks on the United States]. The World Bank calculates that Mexico has exhausted any benefits it secured from NAFTA and expects the decline in employment in the maquiladora sector to accelerate.

Other emerging countries are elbowing their way to the top of the list of most profitable production centers. As the World Bank points out, wages in Mexico are four times higher than in China. The benefits that Mexico derived from being the first low-wage country to sign a free-trade agreement with the United States are being eroded as other countries make similar arrangements and join the WTO [World Trade Organization].

Mexico held out against Chinese membership of the WTO in 2001. China's accession created fierce competition in the key car, textiles and electronics sectors of its export economy. Since 2003, China has overtaken Mexico to become the second-largest exporter to the United States.

Stagnating Standard of Living

Increased productivity has not raised wages which, despite promises, have shown no convergence with those north of the border. Income disparities in member countries have continued to grow since NAFTA came into effect, most strongly in Mexico. Compared with the numbers for the preceding decade (1984–94), just 10 percent of Mexican households saw their income increase; 90 percent experienced decline or stagnation.

How do ordinary Mexicans survive? Half the working population top up their wages with jobs in the black economy. A third depend upon *remesas*—remittances from family members abroad—which rose from $3.6 billion in 1995 to $23 billion in 2006.

NAFTA's supporters say it should restrict emigration. Former U.S. Attorney General Janet Reno claimed that migration would be reduced only when decent jobs were available in Mexico, and that NAFTA would create those jobs. The reality was different. Emigration rose by 95 percent between 1980 and 1994, but by 452 percent between 1994 and 2006.

The Potential Problems of NAFTA Plus

As a product of the agrarian revolution of the early 20th century, the Mexican Constitution limited or prohibited foreign investment, especially in land. Since NAFTA, foreign companies can hold as much as 100 percent of the capital in Mexican infrastructure, such as airports, roads and railways. The agreement radically changed the landscape, and NAFTA Plus, as it is called, could prove even more radical.

Its official name is the Security and Prosperity Partnership of North America [SPP], and it is an initiative launched at a March 2005 summit in Waco by Presidents George W. Bush and Vicente Fox and Canadian Prime Minister Paul Martin.

They were following the recommendations of the Independent Task Force on the Future of North America, which brings together the Canadian Council of Chief Executives, the U.S. Council on Foreign Relations and its Mexican equivalent, the Consejo Mexicano de Asuntos Internacionales. All three bodies are entirely composed of business interests.

The report, "Building a North American Community," published two months later, made 39 recommendations to establish a single, secure economic space.

A second summit, at Cancún, Mexico, in March 2006, established the North American Competitiveness Council [NACC] of 10 business leaders from each of the countries. It is supported by another council of 200 businesses whose purpose is to establish NAFTA Plus priorities and bring about "deep integration." Elected representatives and independent organizations were not invited to participate.

"The business leaders who make up the NACC have privileged access to every level of the SPP hierarchy," said David Chapdelaine, professor of international relations at the University of Montreal. "The power to make decisions is being delegated to subordinate organizations whose exact composition, along with the place and date of their meetings, has not been made public. This is creating a significant deficit in democratic legitimacy."

The NACC's last report, in February 2007, hailed the SPP as a strategic, realistic attempt to improve the economies, security and quality of life of all three countries. It claimed that businesses could improve quality of life by creating secure, transparent borders within North America, alongside secure access to profitable energy.

Only goods and natural resources (aqueducts, oil and gas pipelines, transport) will enjoy freedom of movement. The NACC is calling for the oil and gas markets to be opened up and has suggested that Mexico partially privatize Pemex, the state-owned petroleum company, and break it up by giving off its natural gas activities.

This year, the Mexican congress will discuss a constitutional reform bill allowing the partial privatization of Pemex [the bill passed in October 2008]. Mexican farmers might have some thoughts about how that will enhance the quality of life in North America.

> "To the U.S. companies who run ma-
> quiladora factories, the workers are ex-
> pendable and only the financial invest-
> ment is important."

NAFTA Promotes the Exploitative Maquiladora System in Mexico

Mike Westfall

Mike Westfall is a contributor to the Cutting Edge and other news websites. He writes primarily on labor issues. In the follow-ing viewpoint, Westfall condemns the maquiladora factory sys-tem in Mexico, a branch of American industry that utilizes Mexican plants to assemble US brand-name products—all in the name of free trade. In Westfall's opinion, the opening up of Mexican industry under the North American Free Trade Agree-ment (NAFTA) has done little to help relieve Mexican poverty and unemployment. Instead, Westfall asserts that US companies simply built maquiladora plants south of the border, hired cheap Mexican labor, and shipped all finished products back to America for global distribution. The author claims the plants pay starva-tion wages and are rife with instances of rape and other human

Mike Westfall, "Maquiladoras—American Industry Creates Modern-Day Mexican Slaves," The Cutting Edge, June 8, 2009. Copyright © 2008 by TheCuttingEdgeNews .com. Reproduced by permission of the author.

rights abuses. He believes American consumers should know that many of the products they buy are produced under slave-like conditions and should take action to end the maquiladora system.

As you read, consider the following questions:

1. What percentage of maquiladora-made goods return to the United States for sale, according to Westfall?

2. As Westfall writes, about how many maquiladora plants existed in Mexico in 2009?

3. According to the author, how many maquiladora factories was General Electric running in 2006?

American manufacturing industries do not belong to corporations alone and are a prized national asset. They have given us our high standard of living, our power and respect in the world, been a model for the rest of the world to imitate and allowed us to out-produce our enemies during wartimes. Without them, America loses.

But from our nation's first colonies, there have been opportunists who have exhibited a penchant for using racism, elitism and the rules of the marketplace jungle to exploit fellow human beings to enrich themselves. Wealthy Southern plantation owners and other prosperous business leaders of their day introduced African slaves to the Colonies in the 1600s. By 1860 the South had over 4 million slaves who were bought and sold at auctions like livestock. They labored in the fields and elsewhere—producing products for the benefit of their masters. They received no wages, were denied civil rights and they and their families were at the absolute mercy of those masters who owned them.

While slavery is illegal in the United States today, it does come in other forms. That same old U.S. entrepreneurial insatiability for financial gain, regardless of the human cost, is now being exported together with once middle-class American jobs to other less-fortunate nations.

The NAFTA Disaster

Industrial globalization has contributed to the initiation of shockingly cheap offshore product production in places like China, which surpasses Mexico's deplorable low-cost labor status. Mexico, because of its close geographic proximity to the United States, has been particularly targeted by U.S. industry for wage-slavery and consequential human rights violations.

The term for this . . . neo-slavery is *maquila* or *maquiladora*.

A Mexican maquiladora factory allows duty-free temporary importation of machinery, parts and materials to Mexico as long as the produced goods do not remain in Mexico. About 90 percent of what is produced in these maquiladora factories returns to the United States. Companies such as auto, clothing, toy, electronics and others transport their raw materials and/or disassembled parts to these factories, and the Mexican workers labor to complete the manufacturing processes. The products are then returned with very little duties, tariffs, taxes and labor costs to places like Ford, General Motors [GM] and IBM or to the shelves of mega-stores like Kmart and Wal-Mart.

The full impact of the maquiladora concept kicked in with the North American Free Trade Agreement, NAFTA. This treaty was designed to enact special protections for financial interests at the expense of labor in the three nations of Canada, Mexico and the U.S.

Both the Republicans and Democrats jointly supported NAFTA, and it was signed into law under President [Bill] Clinton. It began in January of 1994 and triggered an immediate flooding of U.S. investment into Mexico to build more maquiladora factories. Ross Perot, who opposed NAFTA and ran against Bill Clinton for president, said that the "giant sucking sound would be the jobs heading south to Mexico."

NAFTA has been a disaster for the working people and the communities in which they live in all three nations. Today we clearly see that the results of NAFTA have led to a much weaker America with devastated and shuttered manufacturing communities. Mexican wages have dropped, and almost 20 million more Mexicans now live in poverty. American business leaders have been quick to seize upon the opportunity to take advantage of these desperate workers.

It is common knowledge that many U.S. politicians get hefty campaign contributions from industry. The only NAFTA winners have been the companies and politicians.

There are about 3,000 high-profit maquiladora factories along the 2,000-mile U.S.-Mexican border with over 1 million Mexican workers. As of 2006, maquiladoras accounted for 45 percent of Mexico's total exports.

Subjugation and Exploitation of Mexican Workers

The impoverished maquiladora workers really have few choices and are forced to choose between working for starvation wages and not having employment at all. A husband and a wife working full-time jobs in these factories still cannot earn enough money to decently support a family of four. It is economic subjugation. In too many instances, workers put in grueling 10-hour shifts 6 days a week doing difficult unhealthy jobs at an unreasonable work pace, often around hazardous and toxic elements.

During the 1980s, the American auto industry [was] beginning to shift large numbers of America's premier jobs to oppressed foreign workers. Labor activists began speaking out and taking groups of autoworkers to Detroit to stage protests and demonstrations. They did TV and radio shows and confronted GM's CEO Roger Smith at GM stockholder meetings. They raised issues such as corporate restructuring that was done without regard to social consequences, the practice of apartheid in GM's plants in South Africa or the exploitation of foreign workers.

On the stockholder floor, labor activists would challenge and debate Smith and tell him that his Mexican workers were falling over on the assembly lines from hunger. He once shot back that wasn't true and claimed that GM was furnishing one meal per day to these workers. That statement was immediately picked up and then quickly forgotten by the national press. The truth was that GM was having a yearly labor turnover rate of almost 90 percent, because workers couldn't afford the meager costs necessary for work including food, clothing and transportation expenses.

Maquiladora plants in general have an especially dismal record of exploitation relative to women and children. It has not been uncommon to find children as young as 12 years old working in these factories under forged documents.

In 1999 the net wage for the average maquiladora worker was $55.77 per week, after 4 percent union dues of $2.32. The weekly minimum living expense for one worker was $54. In addition to the pathetic wages and disregarded labor standards, the living and health conditions around these maquiladora factories are beyond belief.

A recent *New York Times* article said that because these workers have no financial resources, a nutritious meal for their family is an unattainable luxury. Many live in a squalid grid of dirt streets, rotting garbage, swamps of open sewers with unsafe water, overburdened or nonexistent schools and violence against the women.

Unhealthy Working Conditions

A December 2007 *Global Exchange* article, discussing maquiladoras since NAFTA, discussed how worker settlements were sprouting up around these factories with housing made from cardboard, sticks and sheet metal. These shanties had neither sufficient clean water nor adequate sewage systems. The article talked of sweatshop blue jean maquiladoras making millions of dollars off their workers, including children under the age of 11, and of young women workers suffering sexual harassment. It told of laborers putting in 12-hour workdays producing thousands of pairs of Polo Ralph Lauren, Tommy Hilfiger and Wrangler jeans per week for weekly wages of 700 pesos ($53 U.S.). These jeans were being sold in Los Angeles stores for 1,000 pesos ($75 U.S.) per pair.

These jean factories pollute the local water. The stone washing and bleaching leaves highly toxic wastewater with heavy metals in the effluent. The article stated that the runoff makes the nearby farm fields become iridescent and radiates a metallic blue because of this chemical runoff.

An article titled "Maquila Neoslavery" by journalist and human rights activist Gary MacEoin in the *National Catholic Reporter*, noted that a typical maquila 9-hour day quota for a woman is to iron 1,200 shirts. MacEoin said "few survive the unhealthy working conditions, poor ventilation, verbal abuse, strip searches, and sexual harassment for more than six or seven years."

Dr. Ruth Rosenbaum, executive director CREA [Center for Reflection, Education and Action], said the wages do not enable them to meet basic human needs of their family for nutrition, housing, clothing, and non-consumables and that one maquiladora worker provides only 19.8 percent of what a family of four needs to live.

Author Rachel Stohr talked of the brutal treatment, the wage slavery, of how the Mexican government gains economically from these factories and how the enforcement of Mexican labor laws is just not happening in a 2004 University of New Mexico story.

To the U.S. companies who run maquiladora factories, the workers are expendable and only the financial investment is important. According to Rev. David Schilling, director of

ICCR's [Interfaith Center on Corporate Responsibility's] Global Corporate Accountability Program, for years religious institutional investors have been pressing corporations to pay their Mexican employees a sustainable living wage.

Martha Ojeda, director of Coalition for Justice in the Maquiladoras, said "they work long productive hours for the world's biggest corporations and still cannot provide the most basic needs for their families, they cannot afford to consume the items they produce."

Brian Chasnoff wrote in the *Comité Fronterizo de Obreros* that the Immigration Clinic of San Jose says that it hears of so much rape in the maquiladoras that it is disgusting.

A History of Corporate Abuse

Some of the companies who participate in this elitism and human deprivation are historically not strangers to oppression and exploitation. Award-winning author Edwin Black, in his new book *Nazi Nexus*, discusses the complicity of American companies like Ford, General Motors, and IBM with their connections to Hitler's regime against the Jews beginning in the 1930s. Interestingly these same three companies have continued to find themselves on the wrong side of the moral table throughout their histories, as evidenced with the current accusations being directed against them for practicing apartheid in South Africa and also with the maquiladora factories they each run in Mexico.

As of the writing of a December 1998 *BusinessWeek* article called "Mexican Makeover," IBM had boosted exports from $350 million to $2 billion.

Ford has maintained a presence in Mexico since 1925. In David C. Korten's book, *When Corporations Rule the World*, he told of how in 1987 Ford Motor Company tore up its Mexican union contract, fired 3,400 workers, and cut the already low wages by 45 percent. When Ford workers rallied around dissident labor leaders, gunmen hired by the official government-dominated union shot workers at random.

General Motors is another key industry titan named in Edwin Black's *Nazi Nexus*. A July 9, 1997, Campaign for Labor Rights newsletter in Washington, D.C. stated that the Coalition for Justice in the Maquiladoras was protesting the firing of 33 GM *maquila* workers for a work stoppage due to wage issues. These desperately poor workers agreed to a settlement with a mere $32 in food coupons redeemable in local stores. GM had six plants at this location. This newsletter stated that GM's maquila workers are faced with a brutal economic crisis and the less than $40 per week wage that they took home didn't cover the basic nutritional requirements of their families. The newsletter stated that these workers were some of the most productive industrial workers in the world, and General Motors employed 70,000 of them in maquiladoras around Mexico.

There is a long list of U.S.-based multinationals including Fortune 500 companies who run Mexico's maquiladora factories. Mexico's Maquila Portal stated how many factories and how many workers were involved in 2006.

Some examples were . . .

- Delphi, which split off from General Motors and remains a major auto supplier, has 66,000 workers and 51 maquiladora factories
- Lear Corporation, 34,000 workers and 8 factories
- General Electric, 20,700 workers and 30 factories
- Jabil Circuit, 10,000 workers and 3 factories
- Visteon, 10,000 workers and 16 factories
- Whirlpool, 7,500 workers and 5 factories
- Emerson Electric, 5,678 workers and 7 factories

- Motorola, 5,290 workers and 2 factories

- Honeywell, 4,900 workers and 3 factories

- Plantronics, 3,600 workers and 5 factories

- Bose, 2,900 workers and 2 factories

- Mattel, 2,578 workers and 1 factory

An Environmental Justice Case Study: "Maquiladora Workers and Border Issues" by Elyse Bolterstein, stated that the 2,000-mile border between the United States and Mexico had become what the American Medical Association called "a virtual cesspool and breeding ground for infectious disease." The article says workers had to endure terrible working conditions that included exposure to potentially hazardous materials and that one-fifth of a surveyed group of workers suffered from work-related illnesses. The article stated that loosely enforced Mexican environmental laws and a lack of suitable waste storage caused the border to be among the most polluted areas in Mexico. Border residents are exposed to high air pollution levels, and there are considerable toxic materials dumped into the Rio Grande, poisoning the communities along the river and causing illnesses like hepatitis.

Consumers Should Take Action

Consider the hopeless plight of these hurting Mexican families for a moment. As U.S. industry has exported jobs to Mexican workers, who they expect to work for starvation wages, these same workers have been exporting themselves to the United States. Jeffrey Passel, a demographer at the Pew Hispanic Institute, says they want to come here legally to make a decent living, but their circumstances are so harsh that these people are jumping the fence to come here illegally.

The corporations' public relations departments counter the reality of their behavior by arguing that maquiladora workers are not the least-paid workers in Mexico, and therefore the companies have every right to demand low wages and extract what they can from these vulnerable people. They say their own government condones the maquiladora system.

Thinking, compassionate consumers who buy these companies' products don't want to support this exploitation and the despicable human rights violations. The next time they put on their Wrangler jeans, consumers should consider the grueling hours, the hunger, the sexual harassment of the women, the stolen lives of the children and the destitution of the workers in the various maquiladora garment factories.

When they buckle up their children in their automotive seat belts, they need to think of the Mexican worker who made that seat belt and cannot afford an education or decent home or future for their children. The next time they buy their grandchild a Mattel toy or sweatshop Barbie from the world's largest toy maker, they need to consider not only the company's oppressed workers in Mexico and China, but also the recent recalls over safety concerns over its foreign-produced toys.

Yes, we all need to think about this because when we purchase the products produced by demoralized workers, we are not only losing American middle-class jobs but also directly supporting this neo-slavery.

The World Will Remember America's Role in the Maquiladora System

In civilized nations there are minimum-wage laws, child-labor laws, health and safety laws, environmental laws and laws against sexual abuse and exploitation. Politicians actually have a desire to protect their workers. U.S. politicians should be ashamed of themselves for allowing products to come into this country that were made by exploited workers. Instead, they, with their corporate colleagues, have enabled it while slicing U.S. manufacturing capacity and painfully eliminating good-paying middle-income jobs. These politicians have substantially weakened America.

The irony is that while we wish to buy products made by workers who are not exploited, the day is fast approaching when the only products you can find made in the U.S.A. will be in the antique malls.

The companies professed that these factories would benefit everyone connected to them. They lied.

Raising wages, which improves living standards in poor countries, is in direct opposition to their best interests, and social responsibility just isn't a consideration. Sooner or later, as the rest of the world becomes more powerful and the U.S. becomes less dominant, the world will remember the abuse that U.S. corporations and political leaders visited upon them. There could be retribution to pay.

The successful double-talk of Wall Street and powerful industries arguing that blind, open free trade, at the expense of powerless workers and their families, would promote democracy and improve living conditions has been proven false. The exploitative maquiladora system is the kiss of death to all of the workers of the world.

| "*Maquiladoras still have great possibilities for sustained future growth of the Mexican economy.*"

The Maquiladora System Is a Beneficial Part of the Mexican Economy Under NAFTA

Joseph Heinzman Jr. and Gian Marco Valentini

In the following viewpoint, Joseph Heinzman Jr. and Gian Marco Valentini report that despite declining employment levels due to various financial downturns, the maquiladora system is still a powerful and growing production force in Mexico. According to the authors, the maquiladoras—American-owned factories in Mexico that produce goods for distribution in US markets—take advantage of the North American Free Trade Agreement (NAFTA) to manufacture or assemble products and ship them across the border without paying tariffs. In this way, the maquiladoras can compete in some markets with countries like China that still have to add the cost of import duties onto products sold in the United States. Heinzman and Valentini claim that as the demand for these Mexican-produced commodities grows, the

Joseph Heinzman Jr. and Gian Marco Valentini, "Maquiladoras: An Important Asset for Mexico's Economy," *International Business & Economics Research Journal*, vol. 7, no. 6, June 2008. Copyright © 2008 by The Clute Institute. Reproduced by permission of the authors.

maquiladoras are able to employ more workers and pay better wages than many impoverished Mexicans currently earn. Heinzman is the program chair of the business administration program at Hodges University in Florida. Valentini was a business administration graduate student at Hodges when this piece was written.

As you read, consider the following questions:

1. According to studies conducted by the Federal Reserve Bank of Dallas and cited by the authors, maquiladora products make up about what percentage of Mexico's total exports?

2. As the authors state, what was the gross US-dollar value of maquiladora production in 2005?

3. In what arenas of production do Heinzman and Valentini claim the future potential of the maquiladora system lies?

M aquiladoras are manufacturing firms, operating in Mexico under special customs treatments. Because of this special customs regulation, American companies can send raw materials, equipment, and machinery to maquiladoras without paying any import duty. Once in Mexico, raw materials and other supplies are processed and assembled. Finally, the finished goods are sent back to the United States or to foreign markets.

The maquiladora program, also known as Mexico's Border Industrialization Program (BIP), started in 1965, about 1 year after the termination of the Bracero Program, a plan established by the American government to attract Mexican workers in the agricultural sector. With Mexico's Border Industrialization Program, the Mexican government tried to reach the two following goals:

- Persuade foreign investors to build manufacturing companies in the country.

- Give a job to about 4 million Mexicans who were returning to their own country after the termination of the Bracero Program.

In other words, the BIP can be viewed as the extension of the Bracero Program to the industrial sector. Initially, the BIP did not obtain the success that the Mexican government was expecting. Mexican labor wages were still too high to be attractive and competitive. Initially, European and American investors opened only a few factories in Mexico.

The situation changed drastically in 1982 when the Mexican currency experienced a strong devaluation. As a consequence of devaluation, wages dropped considerably and the BIP registered a remarkable growth. . . . Mexico's share of United States imports increased considerably after 1965, when Mexico's share of United States imports rose from a simple 0.52% in 1965, the year when the BIP was launched, to 17.67% in 1986.

Maquiladoras Under NAFTA

In these plants, materials and supplies are processed, and the final products are sent back to the United States or to foreign markets.

Maquiladoras benefit from a special customs treatment. Specifically, supplies, materials, and equipment imported to a maquiladora from a North American Free Trade Agreement (NAFTA) country are not subjected to customs duties in Mexico. In addition, resources imported from non-NAFTA countries are still exempt from Mexican import duties, if the final products are exported to a non-NAFTA market. Non-NAFTA originating supplies, equipment, and materials are subjected to Mexican import duties, if the final goods are successively exported to a NAFTA market.

There are basically no restrictions on the types of products that can be manufactured in a maquiladora. The only limitations regard the production of weapons and the use of radio-active materials. In this case, investors must attain a special authorization from the Secretary of Defense and from the Mexican nuclear regulatory agency. . . .

The Impact of Maquiladoras on the Mexican Economy

There is no doubt that maquiladoras represent an important aspect of the Mexican economy. In fact, the strategic proximity to the United States allows maquiladoras to introduce the products manufactured into the American markets in real time. In addition to that, Mexican labor wages are much lower than both the American wages and the wages of many other countries. Low Mexican wages can be considered responsible for the great success obtained by the maquiladoras.

Chart 1 [the sidebar in this viewpoint] indicates the maquiladora industry and its impact on the Mexican economy by showing the salaries received by Mexican workers employed in maquiladoras during the past few years—the salaries received by maquiladora employees are extremely low. In particular, maquiladora wages are much lower than American wages. As the graph shows, between 2000 and 2005, the maquiladora wages were below $2 per hour, less than half of the minimum wage received by American workers employed in similar industrial sectors. In addition, it is important to observe that maquiladora wages did not increase in total between 2000 and 2005. Wages actually registered a sharp decline. That is why many American companies entered into the maquiladora program in Mexico—in the attempt to reduce their production costs.

Job Creation

One of the major results of maquiladoras on Mexico's economy is the creation of jobs for the Mexican workforce. In fact, it is possible to classify the maquiladora industry in eight

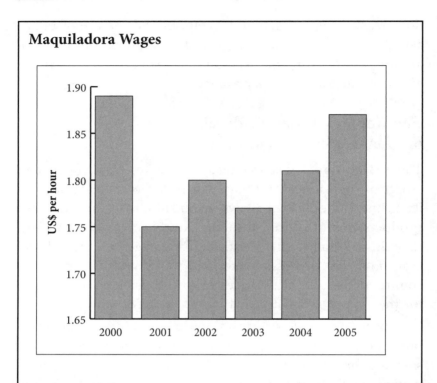

Maquiladora Wages

TAKEN FROM: Joseph Heinzman Jr. and Gian Marco Valentini, "Maquiladoras: An Important Asset for Mexico's Economy," *International Business & Economics Research Journal*, vol. 7, no. 6, June 2008.

different sectors: furniture, electrics and electronics, transportation, textile, chemical, machinery, services, and others. . . .

It is possible to observe that the employment rate dropped between 2000 and 2002. . . . The contraction was due to the problems that the American economy was facing. However, in the last few years, the employment rate [rose] again, showing that the maquiladora industry is still very active and competitive. . . .

The textile sector registered the most significant decline of employment. This contraction is probably due to the competition with China, Bangladesh, and other Asian countries that are becoming more competitive in the international markets.

In the remaining sectors, the employment rate has been constantly growing over the first few years of the new millennium. Such important data can be interpreted as a signal of vitality of the maquiladora industry after the drastic reduction of workers at the beginning of 2000. In particular, both the chemical and transportation sectors registered the most remarkable increase in employment in the past few years.

The creation of job opportunity is not the only impact that maquiladoras have in Mexico. Products manufactured in maquiladoras are exported to the United States and in other international markets, thus improving Mexico's balance of payments. This movement of goods from Mexico to other countries generates a huge amount of money that flows into Mexico's economy. Several studies conducted by the Federal Reserve Bank of Dallas show that maquiladoras account for about half of the Mexican exports. In particular, a recent investigation indicates that in 2006 the maquiladoras were responsible for about 46% of the total of Mexico's exports.

It is necessary to take into consideration the maquiladoras' gross production in order to have a better understanding of the important role that maquiladoras play in the Mexican economy. Chart 2 [not included in this viewpoint] shows the maquiladora gross production in the past few years. This indicates a positive trend of the maquiladoras' gross production during the past six years. In particular, in 2005 the gross production reached $105.4 million. This trend, in association with the increase of the employment rate, supports a prediction that maquiladoras will probably continue to experience a positive growth in the near future.

Another important consideration is the amount of United States dollars that the maquiladora industry generates with its exports. This information is particularly important when compared with the amount of money that non-maquiladora companies are able to create in Mexico. Chart 3 [not shown] compares the exports of maquiladoras and non-maquiladora firms.

The data in Chart 3 indicates that since 1997 the maquiladora industry accounts for about 50% of the Mexican national level of exports. In particular, during the past 10 years, the maquiladora exports increased constantly.

Future Predictions

This study did not predict the future of the maquiladora production based on statistically available information, but the growth trend is fairly steady and there is no indication of any rapid growth in the near future. It is likely that slow, steady growth in the chemical, electronics, and service areas will prevail.

The government of Mexico needs to address the future growth and direction of the maquiladora industry. Low-cost maquiladora manufacturing in the automotive and aerospace industry, products requiring quick reaction production and delivery, and physically large products are on the rise and the future potential lies in these arenas. Products that are cheap to manufacture, inexpensive to transport, and have steady production and delivery requirements will be sent to China by US manufacturers rather than to Mexico. The political environment requires a close scrutiny by academia.

Maquiladoras are a very important part of the Mexican economy. Low wages, the strategic geographic proximity with the American markets, and the less problematic linguistic and cultural barriers contribute to the success obtained by maquiladoras.

From the information collected and explored in this [viewpoint] it is possible to conclude that the maquiladora industry has been experiencing a positive growth since the depreciation of the Mexican currency. In fact, the employment rate in the maquiladora industry has been growing since the crisis of the beginning of 2000. In addition, maquiladoras are able to generate an amount of United States dollars in exports that accounts for about 50% of the national total exports. All of that supports the conclusion that maquiladoras still have great possibilities for sustained future growth of the Mexican economy.

> *"Contrary to NAFTA proponents' pre-dictions, the treaty became an impor-tant source of pressure on Mexicans to migrate."*

NAFTA Is Responsible for Increasing Mexican Emigration

David Bacon

A former labor organizer, David Bacon currently works as a writer and photojournalist. He is the author of Illegal People: How Globalization Creates Migration and Criminalizes Immi-grants. *In the following viewpoint, Bacon accuses the North American Free Trade Agreement (NAFTA) and other globaliza-tion policies of destroying Mexico's price protections for nation-ally produced products, putting millions of farmers and factory hands out of work, and compelling many of those unemployed to seek work in the United States. In Bacon's estimation, NAFTA creates displaced workers—a boon to US industries and maqui-ladora plants that rely on large, low-wage labor pools, but a tragedy for Mexican workers who wish to see their own country's standard of living improve. More worrisome to Bacon is his be-*

David Bacon, "Displaced People: NAFTA's Most Important Product," *NACLA Report on the Americas*, vol. 41, no. 5, September–October 2008. Copyright © 2008 by NACLA Re-port on the Americas. Reproduced by permission.

lief that US immigration policy condemns these undocumented workers as illegal aliens, thus depriving them of labor rights and citizenship rights, while clearly tolerating the need for these workers and the benefits they provide to the economy. He maintains that US workers should stand in support of these migrants because only through solidarity can all laborers be guaranteed a living wage and job security.

As you read, consider the following questions:

1. As Bacon writes, what happened to the government-run CONASUPO stores in Mexico after the enactment of NAFTA in 1994?

2. According to the author, about how many jobs did Mexico lose between 2000 and 2005?

3. What does Bacon say is the main function of US immigration policy?

Since the passage of the North American Free Trade Agreement (NAFTA) in 1993, the U.S. Congress has debated and passed several new bilateral trade agreements with Peru, Jordan and Chile, as well as the Central American Free Trade Agreement. Congressional debates over immigration policy have proceeded as though those trade agreements bore no relationship to the waves of displaced people migrating to the United States, looking for work. As Rufino Dominguez, former coordinator of the Binational Front of Indigenous Organizations (FIOB), points out, U.S. trade and immigration policy are part of a single system, and the negotiation of NAFTA was an important step in developing this system. "There are no jobs" in Mexico, he says, "and NAFTA drove the price of corn so low that it's not economically possible to plant a crop anymore. We come to the United States to work because there's no alternative."

Economic crises provoked by NAFTA and other economic reforms are uprooting and displacing Mexicans in the country's most remote areas. While California farmworkers 20 and 30 years ago came from parts of Mexico with larger Spanish-speaking populations, migrants today increasingly come from indigenous communities in states like Oaxaca, Chiapas, and Guerrero. Dominguez says there are about 500,000 indigenous people from Oaxaca living in the United States, 300,000 in California alone.

Meanwhile, a rising tide of anti-immigrant sentiment has demonized those migrants, leading to measures to deny them jobs, rights, or any pretense of equality with people living in the communities around them. Solutions to these dilemmas—from adopting rational and humane immigration policies to reducing the fear and hostility toward migrants—must begin with an examination of the way U.S. policies have both produced migration and criminalized migrants.

Hoping Free Trade Would Slow Mexican Emigration

Trade negotiations and immigration policy were formally joined together when Congress passed the Immigration Reform and Control Act (IRCA) in 1986. While most attention has focused on its provisions for amnesty and employer sanctions, few have noted an important provision of the law—the establishment of the Commission for the Study of International Migration and Cooperative Economic Development, to study the causes of immigration to the United States. The commission was inactive until 1988, but began holding hearings when the U.S. and Canadian governments signed a bilateral free-trade agreement. After Mexican president Carlos Salinas de Gortari made it plain he favored a similar agreement with Mexico, the commission made a report to the first president George Bush and to Congress in 1990. It found, unsurprisingly, that the main motivation for coming north was economic.

To slow or halt this flow, it recommended "promoting greater economic integration between the migrant-sending countries and the United States through free trade." It concluded that "the United States should expedite the development of a U.S.-Mexico free-trade area and encourage its incorporation with Canada into a North American free-trade area," while warning that "it takes many years—even generations—for sustained growth to achieve the desired effect."

The negotiations that led to NAFTA started within months of the report. As Congress debated the treaty, Salinas toured the United States, telling audiences unhappy at high levels of immigration that passing NAFTA would reduce it by increasing employment in Mexico. Back home, Salinas and other treaty proponents made the same argument. NAFTA, they claimed, would set Mexico on a course to become a first-world nation. "We did become part of the first world," says Juan Manuel Sandoval, coordinator of the Permanent Seminar on Chicano and Border Studies at Mexico City's National Institute of Anthropology and History: "the backyard."

The Flood of U.S. Agricultural Crops Overwhelmed Mexican Farmers

Contrary to NAFTA proponents' predictions, the treaty became an important source of pressure on Mexicans to migrate. It forced yellow corn grown by Mexican farmers without subsidies to compete in Mexico's own market with corn from huge U.S. producers, subsidized by the U.S farm bill. Agricultural exports to Mexico grew at a meteoric rate during the NAFTA years, at a compound annual rate of 9.4%, according to the U.S. Department of Agriculture. By 2007, annual U.S. agricultural exports to Mexico stood at $12.7 billion. In January and February 2008, huge demonstrations in Mexico sought to block the implementation of the agreement's final chapter, which lowered the tariff barriers on white corn and beans.

As a result of a growing crisis in agricultural production, by the 1980s Mexico had already become a corn importer, and according to Sandoval, large farmers switched to other crops when they couldn't compete with U.S. grain dumping. But NAFTA then prohibited price supports, without which hundreds of thousands of small farmers found it impossible to sell corn or other farm products for what it cost to produce them. The National Popular Subsistence Company (CONASUPO)—through which the government bought corn at subsidized prices, turned it into tortillas, and sold them in state-franchised grocery stores at subsidized low prices—was abolished. And when NAFTA pulled down customs barriers, large U.S. corporations dumped even more agricultural products on the Mexican market. Rural families went hungry when they couldn't find buyers for what they'd grown.

Mexico couldn't protect its own agriculture from the fluctuations of the world market. A global coffee glut in the 1990s plunged prices below the cost of production. A less-entrapped government might have bought the crops of Veracruz farmers to keep them afloat, or provided subsidies for other crops. But once free-market strictures were in place, prohibiting governmental intervention to help them, those farmers paid the price. Veracruz campesinos [farmworkers] joined the stream of workers headed north.

NAFTA Reforms Ruin Mexico's Economy

Mexico's urban poor fared no better. Although a flood of cheap U.S. grain was supposed to make consumer prices fall, they in fact rose. With the end of the CONASUPO stores and price controls, the price of tortillas more than doubled in the years following NAFTA's adoption. One company, Grupo Maseca, monopolized tortilla production, while Wal-Mart became Mexico's largest retailer.

Under Mexico's former national content laws, foreign automakers like Ford, Chrysler, General Motors, and Volkswagen were required to buy some of their components from Mexican producers. NAFTA, however, prohibited laws requiring foreign producers to use a certain percentage of local content in assembled products. Without this restraint, the auto giants began to supply their assembly lines with parts from their own subsidiaries, often manufactured in other countries. Mexican auto-parts workers lost their jobs by the thousands.

NAFTA was part of a process that began long before, in which economic reforms restructured the Mexican economy. One major objective of those reforms was the privatization of the large state sector, which employed millions of workers. By the early 1990s the Mexican government had sold most of its mines to one company, Grupo Mexico, owned by the wealthy Larrea family, along with a steel mill in Michoacán to the Villareal family, and its telephone company to the richest person in Mexico, Carlos Slim. Former Mexico City mayor Carlos Hank drove the city's bus system deeply into debt, and then bought the lines in the 1990s at public auction.

Rich Mexicans weren't the only beneficiaries of privatization. U.S. companies were allowed to buy land and factories, eventually anywhere in Mexico, without Mexican partners. U.S.-based Union Pacific, in partnership with the Larreas, became the owner of the country's main north-south rail line and immediately discontinued virtually all passenger service, as railroad corporations had done in the United States. As the Larreas and Union Pacific moved to boost profits and cut labor costs, Mexican rail employment dropped precipitously. The railroad union under leftist leaders Demetrio Vallejo and Valentín Campa had been so powerful that its strikes had strongly challenged the government in the 1950s. The two spent years in prison for their temerity. Facing privatization, railroad workers mounted a wildcat strike to try to save their jobs, but they lost and their union became a shadow of its former self in Mexican politics.

Joblessness in Mexico Forces Migrants North

NAFTA's promise, even with the highly touted maquila [referring to foreign-owned factories in Mexico] industry, of more and better jobs has not happened. Many former Mexican industrial workers are now undocumented migrants in the U.S. working in construction, in meatpacking plants, or washing dishes where they can make more in one hour than in an entire day in a maquila.

Witness for Peace, "Broken Promises: NAFTA at 15," 2009. www.witnessforpeace.org.

After NAFTA the privatization wave expanded. Mexico's ports were sold off, and companies like Stevedoring Services of America, Hutchinson, and TMM now operate the country's largest shipping terminals. As with the railroads, the impact on longshore wages and employment has been devastating. In 2006 spreading poverty and the lack of a program to create jobs and raise living standards ignited months of conflict in Oaxaca, in which stakes and demonstrations were met with repression by an unpopular government. Leoncio Vasquez, an activist with the FIOB in Fresno, California, says, "The lack of human rights itself is a factor contributing to migration from Oaxaca and Mexico, since it closes off our ability to call for any change."

Economic Dependency and Large-Scale Unemployment

In NAFTA's first year, 1994, the Mexican economy lapsed when the peso was devalued without warning in December. To avert the sell-off of short-term bonds and a flood of capital to the north, U.S. Treasury Secretary Robert Rubin engineered a $20 billion loan to Mexico, which was paid to bondholders, mostly U.S banks. In return, Mexico had to pledge its oil revenue to pay off foreign debt, making the country's primary source of income unavailable for social needs, and foreign capital took control of the Mexican banking system.

As the Mexican economy, especially the border maquiladora industry, became increasingly tied to the U.S. market, Mexican workers lost jobs when the market for the output of those factories shrank during U.S. recessions. In 2000–01, many jobs were lost on the U.S.-Mexico border, and in the current recession, thousands more are being eliminated. There is no starker reminder of Mexico's dependency on the U.S. economy.

All of these policies produce displaced people who can no longer make a living or survive as they've done before. The rosy predictions of NAFTA's boosters that it would slow migration proved false. Between just 2000 and 2005, Mexico lost a million and a half jobs, mostly in the countryside. Since 1994, 6 million Mexicans have come to live in the United States. In just five years, from 2000 to 2005, the Mexican-born population living in the United States increased from 10 million to nearly 12 million. With few green cards or permanent residence visas available for Mexicans, most of these migrants were undocumented.

People were migrating from Mexico to its northern neighbor long before NAFTA was negotiated. Sandoval emphasizes that "Mexican labor has always been linked to the different stages of U.S. capitalist development since the 19th century—in times of prosperity, by the incorporation of large numbers of workers in agricultural, manufacturing, service, and other sectors, and in periods of economic crisis by the deportation of Mexican laborers back to Mexico in huge numbers."

NAFTA Encourages Emigration

But from 1982 through the NAFTA era, successive economic reforms produced more migrants. Campesinos who lost their land found jobs as farmworkers in California. Laid-off railroad workers traveled north, as their forbears had during the early 1900s, when Mexican labor built much of the rail network through the U.S. Southwest. The displacement of people had already grown so large by 1986 that the commission established by the IRCA was charged with recommending measures to halt or slow it.

Its report urged that "migrant-sending countries should encourage technological modernization by strengthening and assuring intellectual property protection and by removing existing impediments to investment" and recommended that "the United States should condition bilateral aid to sending countries on their taking the necessary steps toward structural adjustment. Similarly, U.S. support for non-project lending by the international financial institutions should be based on the implementation of satisfactory adjustment programs." The IRCA commission report even acknowledged the potential for harm, noting that "efforts should be made to ease transitional costs in human suffering."

NAFTA, however, was not intended to relieve human suffering. "It is the financial crashes and the economic disasters that drive people to work for dollars in the U.S., to replace life savings, or just to earn enough to keep their family at home together," says Harvard historian John Womack. "The debt-induced crash in the 1980s, before NAFTA, drove people north." He adds that the financial crash and the NAFTA reform engineered by Treasury Secretary Rubin, together with New York's financial expropriation of Mexican finances between 1995 and 2000, once again impelled economically wrecked, dispossessed, and impoverished people to migrate north.

Displacement is an unmentionable word in the Washington discourse. But not one immigration proposal in Congress in 2006 and 2007 tried to come to grips with the policies that uprooted miners, teachers, tree planters, and farmers, in spite of the fact that Congress members voted for these policies. In fact, while debating bills to criminalize undocumented migrants and set up huge guest-worker programs, four new trade agreements were introduced, each of which would cause more displacement and more migration.

Today, displacement and inequality are deeply ingrained in the free-market economy. Mexican president Felipe Calderón said during a recent [February of 2008] visit to California, "You have two economies. One economy is intensive in capital, which is the American economy. One economy is intensive in labor, which is the Mexican economy. We are two complementary economies, and that phenomenon is impossible to stop." When Calderón says "intensive in labor," he means that millions of Mexican citizens are being displaced, and that the country's economy can't produce employment for them. To Calderón and employers on both sides of the U.S.-Mexico border, migration is therefore a labor-supply system. Immigration policy determines the rules under which that labor is put to use.

America's Economy Relies on Displaced Workers

President George W. Bush says the purpose of U.S. immigration policy should be to "connect willing employers and willing employees." He is simply restating what has been true throughout U.S. history. U.S. immigration policy doesn't stop people from coming into the country, nor is it intended to. Its main function is to determine the status of people once they're here. And an immigration policy based on providing a labor supply produces two effects: Displacement becomes an unspoken tool for producing workers, while inequality becomes official policy.

Some 24 million immigrants live in the United States either as citizens or with documents, and 12 million without them. If these migrants actually did go home, whole industries would collapse. And employers benefit from large numbers of undocumented people, since illegality creates an inexpensive system. So-called illegal workers produce wealth but receive a smaller share than other workers in return—a source of profit for those who employ them. No one claims that these excess profits are "illegal" and should be returned to those who produced them. Instead, the producers themselves are called "illegal."

Companies depend not just on the workers in the factories and fields, but also on the communities from which they come. If those communities stop sending workers, the labor supply dries up. Work stops. Yet no company pays for a single school or clinic, or even any taxes, in those communities. In the tiny Mexican towns that now provide workers, free-market and free-trade policies exert pressure to cut the government budget for social services. The cost of these services is now borne by workers themselves, in the form of remittance payments sent back from jobs in Nebraska slaughterhouses, California fields, or New York office buildings.

Former Mexican president Vicente Fox boasted that in 2005 his country's citizens working in the United States sent back $18 billion. The World Bank estimates that in 2006 that figure reached $25 billion. At the same time, the public funds that historically paid for schools and public works increasingly leaves Mexico in debt payments to foreign banks. Remittances, as large as they are, cannot make up for this outflow. According to a report to the Inter-American Development Bank, remittances accounted for an average of 1.19% of the gross domestic product between 1996 and 2000, and 2.14% between 2001 and 2006. Debt payments, however, accounted for a good deal more. By partially meeting unmet and unfunded social needs, remittances are indirectly subsidizing the banks.

Treating Migrants like Slaves

At the same time, companies dependent on this immigrant stream gain greater flexibility in adjusting for the highs and lows of market demand. The global production system has grown very flexible in accommodating economic booms and busts. Its employment system is based on the use of contractors, which is replacing the system in which workers were directly employed by the businesses using their labor. Displaced migrant workers are the backbone of this contingent labor system. Its guiding principle is that immigration policy and enforcement should direct immigrants to industries when their labor is needed, and remove them when it's not.

Guest-worker and employment-based visa programs were created to accommodate these labor needs. When demand is high, employers recruit workers. When demand falls, those workers not only have to leave their jobs, but the country entirely. Today, employers and the Department of Homeland Security call for relaxing the requirements on guest-worker visas. Although there are minimum wage and housing requirements, the Southern Poverty Law Center report, "Close to Slavery," documents the fact that the requirements are generally ignored. "These workers don't have labor rights or benefits," Dominguez of the FIOB charges. "It's like slavery. If workers don't get paid or they're cheated, they can't do anything."

New guest-worker programs are the heart of the corporate program for U.S. immigration reform, and are combined with proposals for increased enforcement and a pro-employer program for legalization of the undocumented. Proposals based on this three-part compromise are called "comprehensive immigration reform."

"The governments of both Mexico and the U.S. are dependent on the cheap labor of Mexicans. They don't say so openly, but they are," Dominguez concludes. "What would improve our situation is real legal status for the people already here and greater availability of visas based on family reunification. Legalization and more visas would resolve a lot of problems— not all, but it would be a big step," he says. "Walls won't stop migration, but decent wages and investing money in creating jobs in our countries of origin would decrease the pressure forcing us to leave home. Penalizing us by making it illegal for us to work won't stop migration, since it doesn't deal with why people come."

Reforming Free-Trade Policy

Changing corporate trade policy and stopping neoliberal reforms is as central to immigration reform as gaining legal status for undocumented immigrants. It makes no sense to promote more free-trade agreements and then condemn the migration of the people they displace. Instead, Congress must end the use of the free-trade system as a mechanism for producing displaced workers. That also means delinking immigration status and employment. If employers are allowed to recruit contract labor abroad, and those workers can only stay if they are continuously employed, they will never have enforceable rights.

The root problem with migration in the global economy is that it's forced migration. A coalition for reform should fight for the right of people to choose when and how to migrate, including the *derecho de no migrar*—the right *not* to migrate, given viable alternatives.

At the same time, migrants should have basic rights, regardless of immigration status. "Otherwise," Dominguez says, "wages will be depressed in a race to the bottom, since if one employer has an advantage, others will seek the same thing." To raise the low price of immigrant labor, immigrant workers have to be able to organize. Permanent legal status makes it easier and less risky to organize. Guest-worker programs, employer sanctions, enforcement, and raids make organizing much more difficult.

Corporations and those who benefit from current priorities might not support a more pro-migrant alternative, but millions of people would. Whether they live in Mexico or the United States, working people need the same things—secure jobs at a living wage, rights in their workplaces and communities, and the freedom to travel and seek a future for their families.

| "NAFTA-like free-trade and investment agreements neither neutralize nor cause the forces that drive people to migrate."

NAFTA Is Not Responsible for Increasing Mexican Emigration

Demetrios G. Papademetriou

Demetrios G. Papademetriou argues in the following viewpoint that the North American Free Trade Agreement (NAFTA) had no appreciable effect on emigration from Mexico. In his opinion, other forces—including the lure of the relatively strong American economy, the long-established social networks between Mexico and the United States, and the lack of sufficient job creation in Mexico—are more directly responsible for enticing Mexican laborers to make the journey north. Papademetriou even claims that NAFTA—through its hoped-for creation of some jobs in Mexico—may help ease emigration as the treaty's impact is felt over time. Papademetriou is the president of the Migration Policy Institute and a former director for Immigration Policy and Research at the US Department of Labor.

As you read, consider the following questions:

1. As Papademetriou writes, what was the name of the mid-twentieth-century program that allowed Mexican laborers to freely move between Mexico and the United States to work seasonally in America?

2. In 2000, when the Mexican annual GDP growth rate was 6.6 percent, how many jobs did Mexico add to its economy, according to the author?

3. In what year was the Mexican "peso crisis," as Papademetriou states?

The political passions surrounding the United States' ratification of the North American Free Trade Agreement (NAFTA), and the exaggerated claims about the trade agreement's effects, in many ways confused, rather than informed, the discussion about NAFTA's aim. The U.S. debate's progression from the understandable hyperbole that accompanies the "selling" of politically contentious policies to dire "if NAFTA ratification fails" scenarios was particularly unfortunate. Such rhetoric virtually guaranteed that any subsequent assessment of the agreement's value would be burdened by unrealistic expectations in areas that were strictly secondary to NAFTA's goal of promoting trade and cross-border investment by reducing tariffs and other barriers.

Migration may well be one of these areas—although it could hardly be of greater consequence for the Mexican public and, in some ways, the U.S. public. Indeed, an evaluation of NAFTA through the lens of migration is fraught with immense difficulties. Concurrent major economic events in both Mexico and the United States since NAFTA came into effect— ranging from the Mexican economic crisis of the mid-1990s and the *peso's* devaluation to remarkably strong U.S. economic growth later in that decade—as well as migration's deep and structural roots in the two countries' historical relationship, confound the process of isolating and accurately measuring NAFTA's precise effects on migration from Mexico to the United States. Such an evaluation must nonetheless be attempted, if for no other reason than the fact that free trade and migration are so intimately linked in the public's mind. My evaluation will assess whether NAFTA lived up to predictions of the trade treaty's effect on migration, and explore what can be learned from NAFTA when migration is under consideration in future trade negotiations.

NAFTA Has No Effect on Migration

Ten years ago [in 1994], both U.S. and Mexican officials argued passionately that NAFTA, by encouraging job growth in Mexico, would reduce illegal immigration from Mexico to the United States. So far, these hopes seem dashed. Although Mexican job opportunities in the export sector increased (mostly in manufacturing), net job gains have been modest at best, and, depending on the timing of the measurement, even flat. Furthermore, average wages in the two countries have hardly begun to converge. In part because of these factors, but also because of robust U.S. demand for low-wage labor and other structural forces, illegal immigration from Mexico has risen sharply since 1994 despite increasingly vigorous border enforcement efforts that commenced at roughly the same time as NAFTA. Indeed, by most estimates, the population of unauthorized Mexican immigrants in the United States more than doubled between 1990 and 2000 (with most of that growth after 1994), and has continued to grow strongly in the new century.

Is NAFTA, then, responsible for this increase in migration, as some of its critics had predicted? I do not believe so. The analysis points instead to a picture in which the financial crises and restructuring in Mexico that both preceded and followed the trade agreement's enactment, the continuing inability of Mexican job creation efforts to keep up with the million or more new workers entering the Mexican labor force annually, the booming U.S. economy, and the strong migration networks tying the two countries have had a far more powerful effect on migration than NAFTA.

The overarching lesson from the analysis is clear: NAFTA-like free-trade and investment agreements neither neutralize nor cause the forces that drive people to migrate. NAFTA has neither rescued nor gutted the Mexican economy, and net changes in employment during a short but eventful ten years have not been significant enough to offset the pressures and incentives for migration. Policy makers, then, should not expect free-trade agreements to "solve" migration problems. The economic and social realities that drive migration will endure through and behave independently of such agreements. In the end, acknowledging these realities and engaging in the sensible and coordinated—even joint—management of migration may be the only viable option.

Expansion of Legal Migration Channels

Migration management cannot be focused exclusively on controls, however. Managing the migration spigot more effectively implies recognition and regulation of the demand for more permanent immigration and temporary work visas in both countries—in other words, it requires the more thoughtful expansion of legal migration channels and taking joint responsibility for the immigration process itself. This is the only way to do better in the migration area at least until the economic growth that trade agreements and other policy initiatives can deliver in the longer run can modulate the demand on both sides of the migration divide.

On NAFTA's tenth anniversary, however, one additional question is still relevant. Are free-trade negotiations and agreements a valid forum for addressing migration per se? The NAFTA negotiators' answer was a very timid "maybe." The agreement completely ignored the larger issue of low-skill labor migration while allowing professionals in sixty-three occupational categories to accept employment anywhere within the NAFTA space. But such "largesse" was apparently just a short-lived occurrence. In subsequent U.S. free-trade agreements with Chile, Jordan, and Singapore, as well as a Canadian agreement with Costa Rica, the United States and Canada have retreated from this approach. This clearly indicates how difficult the negotiations on the movement of "natural persons" for the purpose of employment are likely to be in negotiations over the Free Trade Area of the Americas (FTAA), the Central American Free Trade Agreement(CAFTA), and the World Trade Organization (WTO).

I argue that the only viable solution to fundamental disagreements over migration in the foreseeable future lies in bilateral and, gradually, regional cooperation. To the extent that NAFTA-like exercises make such cooperation more viable—as NAFTA has done in many ways—free-trade agreements can become down payments on the long-term investment in "habits of cooperation." Indeed, trade agreements should not be seen as the last word on either bilateral or regional relationships, but as part of an ongoing process of engagement. To borrow loosely from Winston Churchill's views about the promise of a united Europe, broad relationships between and among neighbors are living things that grow and adapt in response to shifting on-the-ground conditions. NAFTA-like agreements can thus make important contributions to the growth of more successful "living things," which can in turn set the stage for further cooperation on migration and other deeply divisive issues. . . .

A History of Cross-Border Work

Migration from Mexico to the United States—as it increased throughout the twentieth century—grew geographically dispersed and, as a social and economic force, more permanent in nature. The recruitment and social networks tying the two countries are by now so deeply embedded that migration is an entrenched part of both countries' economies and societies. By the 1940s, well after most other immigration flows to the United States had begun to include large numbers of women, migration from Mexico continued to involve largely the circular movement of male Mexican laborers from the rural states of central Mexico to the U.S. Southwest. In the mid-1950s, at the peak of the special Mexico-United States agricultural labor arrangement known as the Bracero Program (which lasted from about the early 1940s to 1964), more than a half-million Mexican workers were migrating per year to the United States. Yet enough workers were migrating outside the program's parameters that the United States deported more than 3 million Mexicans between 1950 and 1955 without seriously impeding the ability of U.S. farmers to employ Mexican labor.

Permanent Mexican immigration to the United States, relative to the more typical pattern of repeated short trips northward for seasonal work, was still relatively uncommon in the mid-twentieth century despite the fact that the United States' admissions system for permanent immigrants in some ways favored Mexico (and Canada). Specifically, the First Quota Act of 1921 established a national origin-based quota system for the Eastern Hemisphere, while the Western Hemisphere remained unaffected. It was not until the 1965 amendment to the Immigration and Nationality Act that a ceiling of 120,000 annual slots, effective from 1968 to 1978, was designated for the Western Hemisphere, with Mexico and Canada the de facto beneficiaries. Permanent admissions from Mexico yet averaged only some 45,000 per year through the 1960s, in large part due to the preference of Mexican workers for circular migration and rather strict procedural U.S. rules, most notably a labor certification requirement. Thus, in 1960 Mexicans accounted for only 6 percent of the total foreign-born population in the United States.

Over time, these temporary and permanent movements built intricate and durable networks that generated increasing migration flows from Mexico to the United States. In the 1950s and early 1960s, some bracero workers "leaked" out of the agricultural sector and into permanent employment. Each permanent immigrant multiplied the potential immigration from Mexico by enabling family reunification, by arranging jobs for family members and friends, and, in some instances, by financing the unauthorized migration of other migrants and by providing a temporary social safety net for them. By the late 1970s, these networks had matured and had begun to spread. They no longer connected only agricultural areas, but attracted migrants from other parts of Mexico, including some urban areas, and sent them to major cities in the United States, particularly in the Southwest but also in the Chicago and New York metropolitan areas. Mexican migrants filled an increasingly broad range of jobs, moving from the agricultural sector into food processing, low-value-added manufacturing, and personal services. With the capping of certain permanent immigrant admissions from the Western Hemisphere in 1978, demand for family immigrant visas began to exceed supply. Legal permanent immigration from Mexico continued to grow through the 1980s, averaging 65,500 admissions per year from 1980 through 1986. With opportunities for legal admissions remaining grossly inadequate to meet demand, illegal immigration from Mexico continued to grow.

In 1986, the U.S. Congress passed the Immigration Reform and Control Act (IRCA). Among other things, IRCA provided for the legalization of unauthorized immigrants who could show they had been residents in the United States since January 1, 1982, or had worked in U.S. agriculture for a specified time. IRCA also created a system of graduated sanctions for employers who hired undocumented immigrants "knowingly." From 1989 to 1994, almost 2.5 million Mexicans received permanent residency, 2 million of these thanks to IRCA's legalization provisions. The law led to an initial decrease in the stock of unauthorized immigrants, but one of its net effects was to lay the foundation for increased immigration in the future. With IRCA's border-control provisions essentially unfunded until the mid-1990s and its controversial employer-sanction provisions deeply underenforced, illegal immigration resumed. Compounding the problem was IRCA's failure to make provisions to address continuing labor demand by widening legal migration channels. Further, the large number of now-legal Mexican immigrants provided the foundation for increased legal family reunification, but many also likely facilitated the illegal immigration of friends and family.

The integration of Mexican workers into expanding segments of the U.S. labor market had been steadily increasing for well over fifty years prior to NAFTA. In contrast, NAFTA's provisions to integrate the goods-and-services markets of the two countries have been in effect for only ten years. Thus, it is no surprise that free trade has had little effect on the twin pillars of Mexican migration to the United States: intricate networks of social ties and labor market interdependence.

Too Few Jobs Even in the Best of Times

Throughout the 1980s and leading up to NAFTA's implementation, Mexico's demographic changes were putting increasing pressure on the sputtering Mexican labor market. While the rates of Mexican infant mortality and mortality in general steadily decreased, birthrates continued to rise, peaking in 1963. They did not begin to decline significantly until after 1974, when the Mexican government began aggressive family-planning initiatives. Through the 1980s and early 1990s, this demographic momentum translated into a need to absorb an ever-increasing number of new entrants into the workforce each year. In 1988, the annual increase in the population between ages fifteen and sixty-five years reached 1.4 million, and growth in the working-age population plateaued at that figure through 2001.

However, this growth will gradually slow: The population of school-age children has begun to decrease and will continue to do so through at least 2010. Mexico's National Population Council (Consejo Nacional de Población) estimates that the growth in the population of economically active people—those who are working or looking for work—has peaked: The active workforce grew by 6.7 million people between 1995 and 2000, but is expected to grow by only 5.9 million between 2000 and 2005, and 5.4 million between 2005 and 2010. An ever-larger working-age cohort has meant that even during periods of steady growth, Mexico's economy has faced an uphill battle in generating jobs (and wages) sufficient to maintain the standard of living of its people. Only now are the cohorts of young people entering the labor market becoming smaller, giving the economy a chance to catch up.

To demonstrate the power of this demographic momentum during the NAFTA era, consider that when Mexico's real gross domestic product (GDP) was growing at an enviable annual rate of 6.6 percent in 2000, it was only adding about 525,000 jobs in the formal sector; it added about 700,000 in 1999, also a good year for the national economy. However, Mexico's working-age population grew by more than twice as many people in those same two years. Although estimates of the annual growth of the actual workforce vary, it is clear that even in its best years, the Mexican economy left hundreds of thousands of new entrants to the labor force (as well as their unemployed and underemployed predecessors) to choose between the informal sector and, if they had the wherewithal, migration.

Also relevant to Mexico-United States migration is Mexico's continuing process of rural out-migration. Mexico, like many developing and middle-income countries, is experiencing a relentless process of rural out-migration and urbanization—a process that most economists and historians consider a natural part of economic development. In 1970, 41.3

percent of the Mexican population lived in rural areas. By 1990, this figure had dropped to 28.7 percent, and urbanization continued in the 1990s with the rural population accounting for 26.5 percent of the total population in 1995 and 25.4 percent in 2000. Agricultural employment grew briefly in the late 1980s and early 1990s before resuming its downward trend. In some cases, individuals migrated directly to the United States; others chose migration to metropolitan areas in Mexico instead. In the latter case, however, when Mexico's cities could not generate sufficient opportunities for these migrants, many of them wound up undertaking another migration—this time to the United States. Both of these processes—the demographic transition and urbanization—thus provide further reason why it would have been unrealistic to expect NAFTA to have reduced migration pressures in only its first ten years of existence. . . .

The Decline of the Peso and the Lure of the American Economy

NAFTA's entry into force was quickly overshadowed by the "peso crisis" of 1994. The results of the crisis were an immediate devaluation of the peso by more than 50 percent, a 1996 GDP that shrank 6.2 percent from the previous year, an increase in outright urban unemployment from 3.6 percent in 1994 to 6.3 percent in 1995, and a large movement of workers into informal-sector employment. The effects were not unlike those of the 1982 crisis: Large numbers of formal-sector jobs were lost, real wages in Mexico dropped severely relative to those in the United States, and confidence in the Mexican economy was badly shaken. In one public opinion poll taken during the thick of the crisis, in March 1995, only 35 percent of those polled said they thought that economic conditions would improve in the next year.

The response of many Mexicans was similar to that shown in the 1982 crisis: Few jobs in Mexico, high relative wages in the United States, and uncertain prospects for the future added up to good reason to head up the well-trod path northward. Apprehensions along the border jumped in 1995, and continued to increase in 1996.

Similarly, while the NAFTA negotiations probably promoted some of the exuberant investment in Mexico that led up to the peso crisis, the crisis itself cannot be attributed to the trade agreement. Further, the political ties developed in the course of the NAFTA negotiations and the thickening economic linkages secured by NAFTA clearly played a strong role in encouraging the United States to engage in the unprecedented bailout that mitigated the crisis. If it had any effect, NAFTA likely dampened the effects of the economic crisis.

In 1994, real U.S. GDP grew by 4 percent from the previous year, beginning a remarkable period of sustained growth that lasted until 2000. Unemployment stood at 6.1 percent in 1994 and descended to 4.0 percent by 2000, the lowest average rate since 1969. The tight labor market provided ample jobs for low-skilled Mexican immigrants, making them a critical part of the robust growth of many sectors of the U.S. economy and playing a key role in drawing additional migrants to the United States. Of particular note was the increasing importance of Mexican workers in the U.S. personal services sector—a development that provided a strong indicator that the NAFTA-abetted increase in the trade of goods and high-skill, high-value-added services was not going to provide an adequate substitute for migration. . . .

NAFTA and Migration: Promise and Reality

In terms of its effects on illegal migration, NAFTA has been cruel to both its most vocal critics and its most ardent proponents. It has not decimated Mexican employment, but it has not led to dramatic job and wage growth. If anything, it has shifted the Mexican economy slightly toward greater formal-sector employment, leading one to believe that Mexico's disappointing economic performance in the past ten years may well have been much worse without NAFTA.

Migration from Mexico to the United States, both legal and illegal, has continued to grow. In the ten years that NAFTA has been in effect, vastly expanded investment in Mexico and regional trade in goods has not reduced the movement of people—albeit for reasons that probably have as much to do with conditions in the United States as with those in Mexico. The fairest conclusion may be that, ultimately, NAFTA's economic effects have been dwarfed by much more powerful and enduring forces: robust demand for Mexican workers in the United States; enduring and deeply rooted social networks that promote migration; a demographic boom that is still several steps ahead of the employment creation capabilities of the Mexican economy; and an economy that, like those of many developing countries, has, over the past two decades, suffered repeated grave crises and a painful process of readjustment.

Periodical Bibliography

The following articles have been selected to supplement the diverse views presented in this chapter.

David Bacon — "Displaced People: NAFTA's Most Important Product," *NACLA Report on the Americas*, September/October 2008.

Laura Carlsen — "Armoring NAFTA: The Battleground for Mexico's Future," *NACLA Report on the Americas*, September/October 2008.

José De Córdoba and Christopher Conkey — "Mexican Truckers File $6 Billion Claim Against US in NAFTA Spat," *Wall Street Journal*, June 2, 2009.

Economist — "Bringing NAFTA Back Home," October 30, 2010.

Gustavo A. Flores-Macias — "NAFTA's Unfulfilled Immigration Expectations," *Peace Review*, October–December 2008.

Ewell E. Murphy Jr. — "NAFTA and the New Mexican Presidency," *Canada-United States Law Journal*, 2008.

George Philip — "Mexico and NAFTA," *Harvard International Review*, Fall 2008.

Joseph Sorrentino — "'Está Perdido,'" *Commonweal*, February 12, 2010.

Carol Wise — "NAFTA and Mexico: Sorting Out the Facts," *Insights on Law & Society*, Spring 2009.

CHAPTER 3

Is Cross-Border Migration a Problem for the United States and Mexico?

Chapter Preface

A Rasmussen Reports telephone poll in July 2010 found that 68 percent of surveyed Americans favored the completion of a border fence along key illegal immigration routes between the United States and Mexico. Supporters of the ongoing project—which can be traced to the mid-1990s—believe that tall fencing and vehicle obstacles at crossing points in Arizona, California, New Mexico, and Texas have kept down illegal traffic and will continue to do so if the barriers are extended. To defend their claims, many point to surveys of border crossings such as the September 1, 2010, report by the Pew Hispanic Center that determined the number of illegal immigrants living in the United States had dropped to 11.1 million in March 2009 from a high of 12 million in March 2007.

Mexico's president, Felipe Calderón, has been critical of the border fence project since coming to office. While visiting Canada in October 2006, Calderón stated, "Humanity committed a grave mistake in building the Berlin Wall. I'm sure that the United States is committing a grave mistake in building this fence." Calderón's objections stem from his concern that the fencing is forcing Mexicans to cross the border at more remote, arid, and dangerous points along the unprotected desert regions of the American Southwest. The Mexican president has continued to insist that a better way to stop the flow of immigrants is to work with the United States to help bring economic opportunity to Mexico so that the country's labor force does not feel the need to move north to find employment.

US critics have called Calderón's position hypocritical. Some have suggested that Mexico has done little to halt illegal immigration because those workers who find jobs in the United States send money back home, and that helps prop up the Mexican economy. A Gallup poll in September 2009 reported that in 2007—a year before the global financial crisis that limited the funds immigrants could afford to send home—more than $25 billion was sent to Mexico by family members living in the United States. In an early 2010 *Spotlight* report, the Federal Reserve Bank of Dallas claimed the amount still reached $21.5 billion in 2009 despite the financial downturn. The loss of such revenue would significantly slow consumption in Mexico, these critics charge. Other pundits argue that Calderón's concerns about the US fence are disingenuous given the fact that Mexico has begun erecting its own five-hundred-mile fence along the Guatemalan border. While Mexican authorities assert their fence is designed to stop the flow of drugs from South American sources, an Inter Press Service news story from September 15, 2010, cited the head of customs for Mexico's tax administration, Raúl Díaz, admitting that "it could also prevent the free passage of illegal immigrants."

No one is certain that the US-Mexican border fence is alone responsible for the drop in border crossings since 2007. Many experts believe the financial crisis has simply discouraged immigrants from making the trek north in pursuit of jobs that are drying up as US employers scale back their businesses. In the following chapter, *Wall Street Journal* writer Miriam Jordan expounds this view. Her opinion resides among other views that express unease about the problems of cross-border migration and the fence being built to deter it. Some of these commentators maintain that the integrity of the border must be ensured, while others claim the cost in dollars and lives should not be ignored in such momentous policy making.

> "The only travelers who will be inconve-
> nienced by the border fence are people
> trying to enter our country illegally or
> smuggle drugs or other contraband."

The US Border Fence Will Deter Illegal Immigration from Mexico

Tom Tancredo

From 1999 to 2009, Tom Tancredo represented Colorado in the US House of Representatives, where he chaired the bipartisan Immigration Reform Caucus. He unsuccessfully ran for governor of Colorado in 2010. In the viewpoint that follows, Tancredo asserts that concerns over the environmental impact of erecting a fence along the US-Mexican border may be legitimate, but these are not grounds to dismiss the need for the fence. In Tancredo's opinion, local communities can voice their objections and work toward an amicable solution on fence placement, yet it is important to realize the need for the fence is a matter of national security—one that helps define the border and ensure that illegal immigrants will not so easily ignore national boundaries.

As you read, consider the following questions:

1. According to Tancredo, how is the office of Customs and Border Protection trying to minimize the impact of the fence on local residents?

2. Why does Tancredo believe activists who object to the border fence based on its environmental impact are being hypocritical?

3. How does Tancredo dispute the argument that a border wall will separate people from their relatives and business interests on the opposite side?

At an April 28 [2008] congressional field hearing in Brownsville, Texas, on the proposed border fence, a local resident told the visiting panel, "It isn't really a border to most of us who live down here." There are apparently a lot of people in south Texas who believe such things. They see the proposed fence as an unwelcome statement that we really do have a border after all. That's precisely why we need it.

It's really true that some residents in Texas border towns oppose the fence in principle, not because of environmental or property rights concerns. What those opponents are saying is not that they do not want a fence along the Rio Grande. They don't want a border, either.

From the rhetoric of these opponents of the border fence, you might think the Department of Homeland Security is trying to fence the entire 1,950 miles of the southwest border or the full length of the Rio Grande. The current plan being debated is far more modest. By the end of 2008, we will have pedestrian fencing for only 370 miles—less than 20%—and only 65 miles of that is on the Rio Grande. Remarkably, even this pitiful effort is an affront to the sensitivities of the open borders aficionados.

No Easy Escape for Illegal Immigrants

[Border Patrol agents say the border fence's] primary benefit is forcing crossers to commit. In border areas once blocked only by barbed wire, detected groups could easily flee back into Mexico. But now, after jumping the tall fence, they have no place to run if Border Patrol approaches. In other words, the fence is effective at keeping crossers in the country.

Leo Banks, "Border Fence Proving Effective at Southwest Border,"
WeNeedaFence.com, October 2, 2010. www.weneedafence.com.

Legitimate Concerns Should Not Stop the Building of a Border Fence

Obviously, there are some legitimate issues raised by building an 18-foot fence along many miles of previously open land. The office of Customs and Border Protection is trying to place the fence as close to the Rio Grande as feasible—and along existing levees where possible—and trying to minimize the impact on property values and the local agricultural economy. For example, cattle need access to river water, and this need can be accommodated in most places.

A border fence also will inevitably have some environmental impact—on wildlife and wetlands ecology for example—and those impacts can be mitigated to some extent. Yet these logistical issues do not trump the national security and public safety concerns which demand improved border security.

The environmental activists who scream about the possible impact of the fence are hypocritically silent about the degradation caused by the hundreds of pathways and tons of trash left behind by more than one million border invaders annually. Congressman [Raúl] Grijalva of Arizona is proposing legislation to repeal the law allowing the Secretary of Homeland Security to waive environmental impact regulations to expedite the construction of border infrastructure. He believes border fences disturb the natural ecology. Somehow he is oblivious to the damage done to the ecology and habitat by thousands of tons of trash and thousands of human trespassers allowed over the past 20 years by the lack of a fence.

The Border Is a National Concern

The Rio Grande river is the international border not simply of Brownsville and the state of Texas but of the United States. Illicit drugs and illegal aliens, criminals and potential terrorists smuggled across the border at Brownsville, Laredo, Del Rio or El Paso do not stay in those towns; they end up in Tulsa, Charlotte, St. Louis and New York. The residents of border towns do not possess a veto over how we protect our border.

It is particularly outrageous to hear comparisons of the border fence with the Berlin Wall. Such talk reveals a willful ignorance of the Cold War. If Mexico decides to build an 18-foot wall with land mines and machine guns to prevent its citizens from fleeing, that we can call a Berlin Wall. Mexican or American politicians—or religious leaders or news commentators—who voice such tripe need both a history lesson and a public rebuke.

In many border communities the combination of complacency about border security and family ties that transcend borders leads to an arrogance which is quaint but disturbing. Residents with relatives and business interests on both sides of the border insist that they need to travel back and forth freely—for shopping, birthdays, recreational activities, and so forth. Do local residents of Brownsville and McAllen routinely swim back and forth across the Rio Grande after midnight to visit their aunt in Matamoros or a pottery factory in Monterrey? No, they cross legally at the numerous ports of entry, and will continue to do so after the border fence is completed.

On the Mexican side, over six million Mexican citizens possess Border Crossing Cards which allow entry for 72 hours. Any Mexican citizen with legitimate business in Texas has no difficulty crossing the border through a port of entry. The only travelers who will be inconvenienced by the border fence are people trying to enter our country illegally or smuggle drugs or other contraband. The north-to-south smuggling of guns intended for use by the drug cartels might also be slowed by the border fence.

Build the Fence

Disagreement over the optimal placement for the fence and how to mitigate the disruption to the environment is understandable. What is not understandable or acceptable is opposition to the fence based on an ideology of divided loyalties. Many residents of south Texas enjoy the privileges of dual citizenship in the US and Mexico and they move freely—and legally—back and forth across the border. Those residents need to put those divided loyalties aside and recognize the legitimate imperative for secure borders. We can have an honest debate about where to place the fence, but not about the need for fences to help bar illegal entry.

If there are people in Texas who really think there are no significant differences between Brownsville and its "sister city" of Matamoros, or between El Paso and Ciudad Juárez or Laredo and Nuevo Laredo, they probably haven't spent much time south of the Rio Grande lately. A few weeks coping with the lawlessness created by the "Zetas" [militarized armies of drug cartels] and the corrupt local police may change their minds. Meanwhile, most other Americans are saying—Get on with it. Build the fence.

> *"What the tall barrier has done is create a false sense of security for immigration hard-liners while adding to the fears of law-abiding residents along the border."*

The US Border Fence Divides Neighbors and Tears Apart Families

Gebe Martinez

In the following viewpoint, Gebe Martinez claims that while "immigration hard-liners" insist a border fence on the Rio Grande will protect America from illegal immigrants and drug traffic, the reality is that such divisive barriers simply disrupt families with members on both sides of the border and create ill feelings between Mexico and the United States. Martinez hopes President Barack Obama will forgo extending border barriers and instead focus on reform of immigration policy to deal humanely with immigrants already in America and the economic disparity that encourages more illegal immigrants to enter the country. Martinez is a longtime journalist in Washington and a frequent lecturer and commentator on national policy.

As you read, consider the following questions:

1. Reporting on stories he has heard, why does Martinez say legal Mexican American residents of US border towns are reluctant to enter Mexico to see their families or shop?

2. According to a University of Texas research study, why does the border fence unfairly impact the poor on both sides of the fence?

3. What issue did Luis V. Gutiérrez choose to focus on to encourage President Obama to jump-start his promise of comprehensive immigration reform?

B lack steel bars rise from the dry, hard-packed dirt, 16 feet up toward a sky that has no borders.

Though shiny and new, the barrier on the Texas side of the Rio Grande is an ugly symbol of the border wars on the ground.

Congress—responding to voters who are angered by the rising immigrant population in their neighborhoods—ordered the border fence. Now, as the depressed international economies and increased drug cartel violence weaken this nation and Mexico, the barrier is taking on added significance as a shield against Americans' greatest fears.

Families and Communities Suffer

That is not how I view it.

As I approached the international bridge that connects Del Rio [Texas] to Ciudad Acuña, Coahuila [Mexico], I saw a structure that has pierced the friendliness and innocence of the town where I was born.

What the tall barrier has done is create a false sense of security for immigration hard-liners while adding to the fears of law-abiding residents along the border.

America's Great Wall

Like the Great Wall of China, the proposed U.S. border fence is meant to be a barrier against foreigners and undesirable elements, such as terrorists and drug runners. Like the Great Wall, it will be expensive to build and maintain; like the Great Wall, it may indicate a degree of American ethnocentrism [that one's own ethnic or cultural group is superior] and cultural superiority; like the Great Wall, it will be permeable; and like the Great Wall, it may become a portal of commerce and exchange. Unlike the Great Wall, it does not seem poised to become a symbol of American greatness or a tourist attraction.

Helmut Langerbein,
"Great Blunders?: The Great Wall of China,
the Berlin Wall, and the Proposed United States/Mexico
Border Fence," History Teacher, November 2009.

In Del Rio, where a historic partnership with Acuña includes daily commerce, construction of an international dam and meetings between presidents of both countries, there are stories of legal residents who are reluctant to cross into Mexico to see their families or to shop, out of fear they will lose their legal right to return.

The poor on both sides are the ones who will be mostly hurt by the 670-mile fence along the Texas-Mexico border, according to University of Texas researchers. The structure will not even touch the most expensive and revenue-rich parcels of land, according to the human rights study.

Focusing on Comprehensive Immigration Reform

The cold, harsh look of the new fence underscores the mission undertaken by Rep. Luis V. Gutiérrez (D-Ill.) to put a "human face" on the immigration crisis and, thus, pressure President Barack Obama to act this year [2009] to reform immigration laws.

In a series of "family unity" events being held at churches in 20 cities across the country—from Rhode Island to California and Texas—Gutiérrez and local religious and community leaders are gathering testimony from citizens and visa holders whose families have been upended by what they see as overly aggressive immigration enforcement.

Though Obama campaigned for president with an immigration plan that would include border enforcement, tougher employer rules and earned legalization for illegal immigrants, Gutiérrez worries the president's promise may falter because of the deepening economic recession.

"It seemed to members of the [Congressional Hispanic Caucus] that there was a vacuum; how do you continue to build and galvanize the support for comprehensive immigration reform while the White House is silent?" Gutiérrez said. "How do you create support and let the president know there's a community out there that's still very committed and vigorous?"

After reflecting on Obama's 2008 Democratic convention speech, Gutiérrez came up with an answer: to focus on family separations.

In his single reference to immigration as he accepted the presidential nomination, Obama said, "I don't know anyone who benefits when a mother is separated from her infant child or an employer undercuts American wages by hiring illegal workers."

Holding the President to His Pledge

At an event in San Francisco, House Speaker Nancy Pelosi referred to the federal immigration raids that break up families, calling them "un-American," and demanded they be stopped.

Immigration restrictionists mocked Pelosi's comments. Immigration control groups also sponsored an expensive, weeks-long television ad against Gutiérrez, contending his efforts are costing Americans jobs.

But Gutiérrez's work seems to be paying off.

Pelosi's comments reaffirmed her support for broad immigration legislation, once the White House takes the lead.

And in March, Obama strategized with all 24 members of the Hispanic Caucus after receiving from Gutiérrez 5,500 signatures gathered at the rallies.

The president pledged to hold a White House event on immigration by the end of May.

Obama also will travel to Mexico this month [April 2009] to meet with Mexico President Felipe Calderón to discuss the drug war, immigration and trade.

Meanwhile, Gutiérrez and the Hispanic Caucus have the backing of the Congressional Black Caucus, which agrees this is a civil rights issue. Rep. Mike Honda (D-Calif.), head of the Congressional Asian Pacific American Caucus, will join Gutiérrez at a rally in California. Republican Cuban-American lawmakers from Florida also encouraged constituents to attend the Orlando meeting.

No doubt, Obama will continue to hear opposition from immigration hard-liners who demanded the American version of the Berlin Wall.

But not until laws are changed to effectively control illegal immigration—and end the exploitation of workers and the separation of families—can the face of the nation seem more just and not so ugly.

"After a historic immigration wave, many Mexicans and other Latin Americans are preparing to return to their homelands amid the deepening recession here."

The US Economy Is Compelling Many Mexican Immigrants to Return Home

Miriam Jordan

Miriam Jordan is a senior special writer for the Los Angeles bureau of the Wall Street Journal. *She reports chiefly on immigration issues. In the following viewpoint, Jordan states that many Mexican immigrants in the United States are returning to Mexico because of the poor US economy. She claims that high unemployment is significantly affecting illegal workers, forcing many to go back to their homeland to secure some civil benefits—such as free health care—afforded under Mexican law. Jordan also notes that the number of immigrants trying to gain entrance to the United States—both legally and illegally—is on the decline for the same reasons.*

As you read, consider the following questions:

1. According to a study quoted by Jordan, what was the US unemployment rate for foreign-born Hispanics in late 2008?

2. Between January and September 2008, how many Mexicans registered their US-born children for citizenship in Mexico, as the author reports?

3. What is a "matrícula consular," as Jordan describes it?

During a decade in the U.S., Mexican immigrant Linex Rivera gave birth to three daughters, whose American citizenship offered her hope of staying in the land of opportunity. But with job prospects drying up for her husband, Ms. Rivera last week [February of 2009] joined a phalanx of compatriots at the Mexican consulate in Los Angeles inquiring about obtaining Mexican citizenship for their children.

"We are thinking of returning to Mexico and want our daughters to have all the rights of Mexican nationals," says Ms. Rivera, whose children are nine, five and three.

After a historic immigration wave, many Mexicans and other Latin Americans are preparing to return to their homelands amid the deepening recession here. Mexicans who reside in the U.S. sought Mexican citizenship for their U.S.-born children in record numbers last year [2008].

Weak Economy, Fewer Migrants

The recession is hitting Hispanic immigrants especially hard, according to a new report by the Pew Hispanic Center, a nonpartisan research organization. The unemployment rate for foreign-born Hispanics hit 8% in the fourth quarter of 2008, compared with 5.1% in the same quarter a year earlier. During the same period, the unemployment rate for all U.S. workers climbed to 6.5% from 4.6%.

"There is strong evidence that inflows to the U.S. from Mexico have diminished, and the economic distress is likely

153

giving immigrants already here greater incentive to return home," says Rakesh Kochhar, the Pew economist who prepared the report.

The number of people caught trying to sneak into the U.S. along the border with Mexico is at its lowest level since the mid-1970s. While some of the drop-off is the result of stricter border enforcement, the weaker U.S. economy is likely the main deterrent. Border Patrol agents apprehended 705,000 people attempting to enter the U.S. illegally in the 12 months that ended Sept. 30. That is down from 858,638 a year before and from 1.1 million two years earlier.

To be sure, it is difficult to track short-term changes in the population of the estimated 12 million immigrants who are in the U.S. illegally and toil in the off-the-books economy. Some dispute the notion that Mexicans, who flocked here in the 1990s when they could find jobs paying five times as much as they earned back home, are now returning in large numbers. "We believe it is a myth that a lot of Mexicans are going back," said a Mexican diplomat in Washington, who asked to remain anonymous. "But given the economic situation, some of them might be considering it."

Applying for Mexican Citizenship

A host of metrics suggest they are considering it seriously. Between January and September last year, 32,517 Mexicans registered their U.S.-born children for Mexican citizenship at a Mexican consulate, compared with 28,687 for all 2007 and 20,791 in 2006. The 2008 total is likely to be more than 35,000, according to Mexican consular officials.

U.S. nationality has long been regarded as a prized commodity for immigrants from developing countries. Anti-illegal immigrant activists accuse Latin American migrants of giving birth to "anchor babies" in the U.S. in order to secure welfare and other benefits.

Migrants Who Stay in the United States Are Struggling

Many of the Mexican immigrants who remain in the United States are unemployed, work fewer hours or worry about losing their jobs.

Mexican immigrants, no matter what their legal status, are more likely to be jobless than most other workers, studies show. They face longer odds of finding work in the Inland area [in Southern California], where the unemployment rate is nearly 13 percent, among the highest in the nation.

Immigrants are sending less money to family members in Mexico, causing plummeting sales at some Mexican stores that depend on remittance income. Even churches are seeing a drop in contributions, and towns are struggling to continue development programs that immigrant money helps fund.

David Olson, "Reverse Migration: Economy Forces Some Mexican Nationals to Return Home, with Varying Emotions," Press-Enterprise (Riverside, CA), May 23, 2009.

But Mexican citizenship has its own benefits. Having Mexican nationality entitles U.S.-born children of immigrants to obtain health care, education and other benefits, as well as the right to vote, in Mexico. Mexican nationals also don't face restrictions on land and business ownership that apply to foreigners.

Mexican consulates also report they have experienced a spike in applications for a "personal-effects permit" that entitles its nationals to transfer their household goods to Mexico without paying import duties.

Meanwhile, applications for the "matrícula consular," an identity card that Mexicans in the U.S. need to open bank accounts and conduct other business, such as rent an apartment, appear to be declining. Through the first nine months of 2008, 689,150 Mexican adults had applied for the identity card nationwide. That compares with 947,000 for all of 2006.

"They tell me they are registering their children because they are returning to Mexico or making plans to return," said Mexican Vice Consul Federico Bass in San Bernardino, Calif., a consulate that oversees an area home to more than one million Mexicans.

An Uncertain Future

At a Los Angeles-area strip mall, 40 Hispanic immigrant day laborers gathered early in the morning hoping to snare work landscaping, moving furniture or painting houses. By noon, only one had been hired.

"In the old days, you wouldn't find a soul here at this time," said Braulio Gonzalez, a veteran day laborer who still lingered at midday Wednesday. "There are so many more people and so much less work."

At many corners, day laborers who had agreed never to work for less than $15 an hour are underbidding each other when an employer shows up. Mr. Gonzalez says he lost a drywall job to a fellow immigrant willing to work for half that amount earlier this week. "Competition is fierce," says Mr. Gonzalez.

Ms. Rivera and her husband, Felipe Perez, say many of their friends are ensuring their American kids get Mexican citizenship. "Some of them have already left. Others, like us, want to make sure they're ready if we decide to leave," says Mr. Perez.

Mr. Perez, who works as a waiter for a Los Angeles company that caters events for corporations and universities, says he once worked six days a week. Since November, "I've only been working twice or three times a week," he says. "Our savings are shrinking fast."

"For some time now, news reports have been calling attention to the flow of immigrants back to their homelands."

The Return of Mexican Immigrants to Mexico Is Hurting the US Economy

Jeff Jacoby

In the viewpoint that follows, Jeff Jacoby, an op-ed columnist for the Boston Globe, *asserts that concerns over illegal immigration in the United States have eased in recent years because the number of immigrants has declined considerably. Jacoby attributes this decline, in part, to the fact that many Mexican and Hispanic immigrants are returning to Mexico instead of fighting for nonexistent jobs in the United States. Jacoby points out that instead of celebrating the decline in immigrants as a fortuitous occurrence, Americans should realize that a healthy American economy is supported in large part by the presence of many low-skill immigrants—both legal and illegal.*

As you read, consider the following questions:

1. What issue does Jacoby say may have upstaged immigration in the public forum?

2. By what percentage has the number of illegal immigrants declined between 2007 and 2009, according to the Center for Immigration Studies?

3. According to research published by the Cato Institute, how much money would the US economy gain if the government legalized low-skill immigrant workers?

What ever happened to the furor over illegal immigration? Two years ago [in 2007], the denunciation of "crimmigrants" was approaching fever pitch, especially in conservative precincts, and woe betide any candidate who appeared before a Republican audience and failed to denounce "amnesty" with every ounce of conviction he could muster.

Now, however, the hysteria seems to have cooled a bit. There was no bellowing when President [Barack] Obama reiterated during a Mexican summit last month [August 2009] that he intends to press for "a pathway to citizenship" for the millions of illegal immigrants living in the United States. News stories highlighted instead his acknowledgment that overhauling immigration law would have to wait until next year at the earliest.

Perhaps the brawl over the issue has been upstaged by the brawl over ObamaCare [health care reform], in which immigration has been reduced to a supporting role. Or maybe the lowering of the decibel level is a reaction to something else: a significant decline in the number of illegal immigrants living in the United States.

Decline in Immigrants Entering the United States

For some time now, news reports have been calling attention to the flow of immigrants back to their homelands. Recent headlines tell the story: "Bad economy forcing immigrants to reconsider US" (CNN); "More Mexican immigrants returning home" (*Orange County Register*); "Fewer Cubans make crossing to Fla.; economy cited" (Associated Press); "Job losses push immigrants out" (*Chattanooga Times Free Press*).

According to the Center for Immigration Studies [CIS], which favors sharp immigration restrictions, the population of illegal aliens in the United States declined by almost 14 percent, or 1.7 million people, between the summer of 2007 and the spring of 2009. Analyzing Census Bureau data, researchers Steven Camarota and Karen Jensenius calculate that the number of immigrants entering the country illegally has fallen by one-third, while the number returning home has more than doubled. "Both increased immigration enforcement and the recession seem to explain this decline," they write.

Certainly enforcement is up. The Obama administration, like the Bush administration in its second term, has made a point of tightening the border and punishing employers who hire illegals. "The share of the US border that has a fence has increased significantly in the last three years and the number of Border Patrol agents has more than doubled," the CIS report notes. Removal and deportation of unlawful aliens "has increased dramatically," as federal agents have repeatedly raided workplaces where immigrants are employed.

A Poor Economy Means Cuts in Low-Skill Jobs

But as the slew of news stories focusing on the economy suggest, what is primarily driving the immigration outflow is the recession. In good economic times, immigrants pour into the United States; at other times, the influx slows or reverses. It has ever been thus, and—barring the implementation of a border and workplace crackdown more ruthless than anything most Americans would tolerate—ever will be.

During the recent boom, the US economy was creating 400,000 new low-skill jobs per year. Immigrants surged in droves to fill those jobs, most of them illegally since US immigration law provides almost no lawful option for unskilled immigrants with no American relatives. Immigration is a measure of economic robustness, and the news that 1.7 million fewer illegal immigrants live within our borders is a datum to regret, not celebrate.

Research published by the Cato Institute last month debunks the notion that preventing illegal immigrants from entering or working in the United States is good for the economy. "Increased enforcement and reduced low-skill immigration have a significant negative impact on the income of US households," economists Peter Dixon and Maureen Rimmer write. Whatever savings might be achieved in public expenditures "would be more than offset by losses in economic output and job opportunities for more-skilled American workers."

Legalizing low-skilled immigrants, on the other hand, expands the US economy and leads to the creation of new higher-skilled jobs. Result: "significant income gains for American workers and households"—gains the authors estimate at $180 billion a year.

The benefits of immigration, a potent growth hormone, have always outweighed the costs. Men and women willing to uproot their lives, to brave daunting obstacles in order to come to America and work hard, are men and women we should welcome with open arms. Calling them "crimmigrants" won't accomplish anything. Letting more of them enter legally would.

| "U.S. intelligence and law enforcement officials have been warning that the dramatic rise in violence along the southwestern border could eventually target U.S. citizens and spread into this country."

Border Violence Is Increasing

Ben Conery and Jerry Seper

Numerous killings along the US-Mexican border in 2010 have put authorities on both sides on alert. In the following viewpoint, Ben Conery and Jerry Seper report that the intensity of the violence and the increasing number of Mexican victims are the result of drug cartels carrying out assassinations to protect their business. The authors warn that the recent rise in American casualties is symptomatic of the drug cartels expanding their trafficking routes across the border and not hesitating to kill anyone in their way. Though both Mexico and the United States have deplored these tragedies, justice has been slow in catching up with many of the perpetrators, the authors note. Conery and Seper are staff writers for the Washington Times.

Ben Conery and Jerry Seper, "Border Violence Threatens Americans," *Washington Times* online, April 1, 2010. WashingtonTimes.com. Copyright © 2010 by Foster Reprints. Reproduced by permission.

As you read, consider the following questions:

1. In what state was rancher Richard Krentz found slain, as Conery and Seper report?

2. According to the authors, by what percentage had the number of assaults on US Border Patrol agents increased between 2007 and 2008?

3. As of April 2010, the month this viewpoint was originally printed, how many people in Mexico have been killed by drug cartels, according to the authors?

The killings last month [March 2010] in the Mexican border town of Ciudad Juárez of two U.S. citizens, including an employee at the city's U.S. consulate, along with the slaying of an Arizona rancher, have fueled concerns among U.S. officials that Americans are becoming fair game for Mexican drug gangs seeking control of smuggling routes into the United States.

For more than two years, U.S. intelligence and law enforcement officials have been warning that the dramatic rise in violence along the southwestern border could eventually target U.S. citizens and spread into this country. The violence posed what the officials called a "serious threat" to law enforcement officers, first responders and residents along the 1,951-mile border.

The numbers bear out those concerns, according to the State Department: 79 U.S. citizens were killed last year in Mexico, up from 35 in 2007. In Juárez, just across the Rio Grande from El Paso, Texas, 23 Americans were killed in 2009, compared with two in 2007.

Calling on the Government to Act

In response, Arizona Gov. Jan Brewer and Sen. John McCain, both Republicans, have called on the Department of Homeland Security to deploy the National Guard along the Arizona border. Mrs. Brewer said the rising violence showed the "abject failure of the U.S. Congress and President [Barack] Obama to adequately provide public safety along our national border with Mexico."

Rep. Gabrielle Giffords, Arizona Democrat, whose district includes the area where rancher Robert Krentz was killed, said if the slaying was connected to smugglers or drug cartels, the federal government should consider all options, including sending more Border Patrol agents to the area and deploying the National Guard.

Former Rep. Tom Tancredo, Colorado Republican, and former Rep. J.D. Hayworth, a Republican who is seeking Mr. McCain's senatorial seat, joined in the call for National Guard troops to be stationed along the border.

Mr. Hayworth said the federal government should "act now and step up its efforts to secure our borders."

Texas Gov. Rick Perry also has put into play a "spillover violence contingency plan" to address attacks on American citizens in Mexico. The plan increases border surveillance; intelligence sharing; and ground, air and maritime patrols.

A Spate of Killings

A day before the March 13 Juárez killings, Mr. Perry unsuccessfully sought help from Homeland Security Secretary Janet Napolitano to use unmanned Predator drone aircraft and 1,000 additional soldiers for missions on the Mexican border. He said there was a disparity in the amount of federal resources allotted to Texas for border security.

The White House said Mr. Obama was "deeply saddened and outraged" by the killings and had pledged to "continue to work with Mexican President Felipe Calderón and his government to break the power of the drug-trafficking organizations that operate in Mexico and far too often target and kill the innocent."

The latest victims were Lesley Enriquez, 25, who worked at the U.S. consulate in Juárez, and her husband, Arthur Redelf, 30, both U.S. citizens. They were killed March 13 when Mexican drug gang members fired shots at their sport-utility vehicle as they left a birthday party.

Mr. Redelf was a 10-year veteran of the El Paso County Sheriff's Office. Ms. Enriquez was four months pregnant with their second child. The couple's 7-month-old daughter was found unharmed in the back seat.

That same day, Jorge Alberto Salcido, 37, a Mexican citizen whose wife also was an employee at the U.S. consulate in Juárez, was killed when cartel members shot at his car at a separate location, also wounding his two young children. They had attended the same birthday party.

Mr. Krentz, 58, a longtime Douglas, Ariz., rancher, was killed Saturday. He was found by a Cochise County Sheriff's Department helicopter, slumped over his Polaris all-terrain vehicle on his 34,000-acre ranch. His dog also was shot and was critically wounded. The animal was euthanized on Sunday.

Border Gangs Are Active in the United States

Arizona authorities said they think Mr. Krentz was shot by an illegal immigrant. Police dogs followed the tracks of the suspected killer back into Mexico, about 20 miles south. Authorities think the shooter was either a drug cartel scout or a member of a known gang of border thieves that has terrorized the area's remote ranches.

The Krentz ranch sits in an area that has become a lucrative smuggling route for Mexican drug cartels.

"It's a big deal. It's something that could be a turning point here," said Cochise County Sheriff's Office spokeswoman Carol Capas. "People in the area are on heightened alert. They're grief-stricken, saddened, and they're extremely angry."

Two years ago, U.S. Immigration and Customs Enforcement [ICE], the investigative arm of the Department of Homeland Security, said in a report that border gangs were becoming increasingly ruthless and had begun targeting rivals and federal, state and local police. ICE said the violence had risen dramatically as part of "an unprecedented surge."

Last year, the Justice Department identified more than 200 U.S. cities in which Mexican drug cartels "maintain drug distribution networks or supply drugs to distributors"—up from 100 three years earlier.

The department's National Drug Intelligence Center, in its 2010 drug threat assessment report, described the cartels as "the single greatest drug trafficking threat to the United States." It said Mexican gangs had established operations in every area of the United States and were expanding into more rural and suburban areas.

The report noted that adding to the violence were assaults against U.S. law enforcement officers assigned to posts along the southwestern border. It said assaults against Border Patrol agents increased 46 percent from 752 incidents in fiscal 2007 to 1,097 incidents in fiscal 2008—including the January 2008 killing of an agent by the automobile of a fleeing drug suspect and the fatal shooting of another agent in July 2009.

Authorities Issue Warnings to Travelers

Although no arrests have been made in the Krentz killing, there has been an arrest in the Ciudad Juárez killings. The Mexican military detained a member of the Barrio Azteca gang, which works for the infamous Gulf drug cartel on both sides of the border. The suspect was identified as Ricardo Valles de la Rosa, 42, a resident of both Ciudad Juárez and El Paso.

Barrio Azteca is a U.S. prison gang that later found its roots in El Paso and Ciudad Juárez.

The Justice Department declined to comment on the Ciudad Juárez killings; the Department of Homeland Security did not return messages seeking comment.

The Mexican embassy in Washington condemned the killings but did not respond to a follow-up request for comment about whether the Americans had been targeted intentionally. In a statement, it said the Mexican government would "work closely" with its U.S. counterparts "to track down those responsible for these killings so justice can be served."

The U.S. Drug Enforcement Administration [DEA] would not comment specifically on the case but said "the violence we have been seeing is a signpost of the success that our very courageous Mexican counterparts have had in attacking those drug-trafficking organizations."

The drug rings "are acting like caged animals because they are caged," said DEA spokesman Rusty Payne. "They have lost roots, and they have lost control. The Mexican government has gone after them, and this is the reaction from drug organizations that are in disarray."

On March 14, the State Department issued its strongest travel warning to date for U.S. citizens planning on traveling to Mexico. The department also approved the departure of the dependents of U.S. personnel from consulates in the northern Mexican border cities of Tijuana, Nogales, Ciudad Juárez, Nuevo Laredo, Monterrey and Matamoros.

It warned that the cartels are using automatic weapons and grenades, that "large firefights" have taken place in towns and cities across Mexico and that public shootouts have taken place during daylight hours in shopping centers and other public venues.

The department said drug criminals have followed and harassed U.S. citizens traveling in their vehicles, that travelers on major highways have been targeted for robbery and violence and that others have been caught in incidents of gunfire between criminals and Mexican law enforcement.

"While most crime victims are Mexican citizens, the un-certain security situation poses serious risks for U.S. citizens as well," it said.

A War South of the Border

Since January 2008, nearly 5,000 homicides have been committed in Ciudad Juárez alone, making it one of the most violent cities in the world. The bodies of some of those killed have been dumped in schoolyards and other public venues. Many of the victims were ambushed. Others were killed with grenades and AK-47 assault rifles.

Still others have been decapitated, their bodies hung from bridges—along with banners with warning messages from the cartels.

Mr. Calderón declared war against the Mexican cartels in 2006 and has committed more than 40,000 Mexican soldiers to the fight, although the violence continues to escalate. To date, the cartels in Mexico have killed more than 17,000 people.

At the core of the drug fight are the Sinaloa and Gulf drug cartels, along with the Zetas, a group led by former Mexican military officers. They seek to control long-established smuggling corridors into this country, over which billions of dollars in illicit narcotics travel annually.

Secretary of State Hillary Rodham Clinton traveled to Mexico City this month as part of a delegation to underscore concern over Mexico's drug violence.

"These appalling assaults on members of our own State Department family are, sadly, part of a growing tragedy besetting many communities in Mexico," Mrs. Clinton said.

> "The realities simply do not support the rhetoric about public safety in border states."

Border Violence Is Declining

Julianne Hing and Hatty Lee

Julianne Hing is a reporter and blogger for ColorLines, *a magazine that covers racial issues. Hatty Lee is a visual artist and the art production manager at ColorLines. In the following viewpoint, Hing and Lee claim that increased concern in the United States over border violence is unjustified. As the authors assert, violence at the border and across the nation has declined in recent years. The trumped-up fears of rampant murder at the US-Mexican border is the work of politicians who wish to appear proactive to voters on immigration issues, Hing and Lee argue.*

As you read, consider the following questions:

1. According to the authors, why does Texas representative Henry Cuellar believe that more accidental and regrettable deaths have occurred along the US-Mexican border in the past few years?

2. By what percentage did the murder rate in California drop in 2009, as Hing and Lee report?

3. According to the authors, by what dollar amount has immigration enforcement spending increased between 2008 and 2010?

Immigration may be a deeply divisive political discussion, but there's one point upon which everybody from [President] Barack Obama to [Arizona governor] Jan Brewer seem to agree: America's southern border is a lawless, violent land. The guns have followed the premise. Obama has beefed up border cops, sent in National Guard troops and launched unmanned drones—all that's missing are the Marines, for now.

Increased violence has predictably followed the increased militarization. Two border patrol encounters in the past two weeks have ended in the deaths of unarmed civilians, sparking outrage from Mexican authorities and immigrant rights groups who say that Border Patrol officers routinely use excessive force.

On June 7 [2010], a 15-year-old boy named Sergio Adrian Hernandez Huereca from Juárez, Mexico, was shot and killed by a Border Patrol agent at Puente Negro, an international bridge that joins El Paso, Texas, and Juárez. On May 26, a Border Patrol officer at the San Ysidro, California-Tijuana border shot a 32-year-old man named Anastacio Hernandez with a stun gun. The San Diego County coroner has ruled his death a homicide.

Attorney General Eric Holder called the deaths "extremely regrettable," and the FBI formally initiated a civil rights investigation on Friday [June 11, 2010] into the teen's death in Juárez. Texas Rep. Henry Cuellar told *The Hill* newspaper that his subcommittee may investigate as well, but also conceded, "As you have more presence of Border Patrol and other federal officials on the border, you're going to probably run into more types of incidents like that."

Selling Fear of a Lawless Border

Largely quiet on the "incidents like that," however, are the elected officials who have spent the year drumming up reports of border violence to create political space for anti-immigrant policy.

When Arizona Gov. Jan Brewer signed SB1070 [a state law allowing police to ask all detained individuals for proof of citizenship] into state law in April, she described the border as a lawless, violent war zone. "Our international border creeps its way north," she warned. "We cannot sacrifice our safety to the murderous greed of drug cartels." Last week [June 6–12, 2010], a Louisiana sheriff—St. Bernard Parish's Jack Stephens—justified harassing immigrant oil spill workers by asserting that "illegal aliens" were posing as workers to set up gangs in the area.

National Democrats and Republicans alike have echoed the local officials. President Obama implicitly acknowledged the supposed dangers of life at the border when he announced in May plans to send 1,200 National Guard troops and an extra $500 million to the border. That's not heady enough for electioneering [Arizona] Sen. John McCain, who has wedged funding for 6,000 more border troops into the Senate's pending defense authorization bill.

The same week Obama announced his troop increase, Texas Sen. John Cornyn—who wants to redirect $2.2 billion from the stimulus for border security—wrote in an op-ed: "Our porous border endangers every American, yet Washington refuses to make border security a priority." When reporters pressed Cornyn in a phone conference about the violence he so feared, the senator got stuck. "As far as the Texas border is concerned, to my knowledge, we have not had spillover violence, per se," he told reporters. It was actually "the threat of potential spillover violence," he later clarified.

Percent Decrease in Murder Rates Higher in Major Border Cities than National Decrease

According to the FBI's latest report, murder rates declined during the first six months of 2009, compared to the same period in 2008.

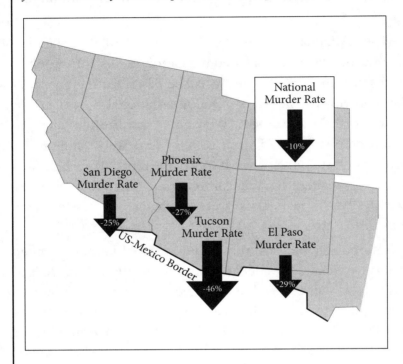

National Murder Rate -10%

San Diego Murder Rate -25%

Phoenix Murder Rate -27%

Tucson Murder Rate -46%

El Paso Murder Rate -29%

US-Mexico Border

TAKEN FROM: Julianne Ong Hing and Hatty Lee, "The Border Violence Lie," Colorlines.com, June 14, 2010. www.colorlines.com.

Violence Is on the Decline

More accurately, it's the perception of that violence. Because the realities simply do not support the rhetoric about public safety in border states. As *ColorLines*' [chart] illustrates, crime in key cities near the U.S.-Mexico border is on the decline—just like it is all over the country.

The murder rate in San Diego, Calif., dropped by 25 percent last year. Phoenix's decreased by 27 percent. El Paso saw a

29 percent drop in murders, bested by Tucson, Ariz., which saw a 46 percent decline in murders. The national murder rate went down just 10 percent from 2008 to 2009.

When it comes to violent crime more generally, all four of these border cities hover around four to six violent crimes per capita, just under the national average of 6.6.

"[Politicians] are creating the artificial reality that the border is out of control, that it spills over. None of that is true," says Fernando Garcia, the executive director of the El Paso-based Border Network for Human Rights. "We have a very sustainable sense of security in the community, good relations with local law enforcement."

"There is a perception of the border that whatever ails the U.S. as a country has to come from the outside rather from looking internally," adds Maria Jimenez, an immigrant rights organizer who works with America Para Todos in Houston. The expectation that more militarization will make the border safer is "unfair to Border Patrol and Customs people, too," Jimenez says.

The national debate around border security is a classic case study in the ways that a twisted narrative can consume the less dramatic picture of reality. And in so doing, allow politicians to move policy that does not help the communities it's supposed to protect.

Indeed, under Obama's watch, the country now has a record number of Customs and Border Protection officers. Immigration-enforcement spending has skyrocketed from $8 billion in 2008 to $11 billion in 2010.

"How come we need the National Guard?" asked Garcia. "We look around, it's not true. However, it seems that the president and McCain, they have this macho pro-law enforcement attitude. It is really unfortunate, how they are playing with our communities."

> "With all the fuss about how Mexican immigrants are changing the face of American society, it's interesting to note that the same is true in pockets of Mexico from American emigrants."

American Immigrants Are Putting a Burden on Mexico

Marisa Treviño

Marisa Treviño is the founder and publisher of Latina Lista, an online news site featuring a host of commentators focusing on issues that affect Latino communities across the Americas. In the following viewpoint, she maintains that while Americans seem outraged at the influx of Hispanic immigrants crossing the US-Mexican border, few seem aware that many Americans—mostly retirees—are traveling south and taking up residence in Mexico. According to Treviño, many Mexican cities now have pockets of American retirees who take advantage of Mexico's inexpensive health care system, price natives out of real estate, and do not bother to learn Spanish. Noting that these complaints are similar to those leveled at Hispanic immigrants in America, Treviño believes correcting the picture to include US emigrants and the burdens they pose for Mexico will help the public recognize that the issue is two-sided and that policy makers cannot solve immigration issues by blaming immigrants.

As you read, consider the following questions:

1. According to Treviño, what is likely compelling many American retirees to relocate to Mexico?

2. As the author reports, how much is Mexico's annual health care premium?

3. What do officials in San Miguel de Allende estimate the city loses in uncollected tax revenues and fees each year from unlicensed businesses owned by foreigners?

Why is it that in Washington conversations tend to be one-sided?

Take for instance my favorite subject these days—immigration. The focus always centers on Mexican immigrants and their impact on U.S. society. Nobody wants to talk about the flip side of this conversation—that while, yes, Mexican immigrants are coming north, there also are American emigrants going south.

And, according to migration experts, U.S. citizens impact the regions of Mexico they have settled into just as much as Mexican immigrants do here.

Retirees Moving South

Mexican census data show that between 1990 and 2000, the number of Americans in Mexico grew 84.3%.

Professor David Warner of the University of Texas, who studies the integration of the U.S. and Mexican health care systems, says more than 75,000 U.S. retirees live in Mexico.

Many of those Mexico-bound are retirees, 55 and older. It's an interesting contrast to the fact found by the Urban Institute that calculates the overall age of an undocumented Mexican immigrant entering the USA since 1996 is 21.

Just as poor economic conditions are the driving forces behind these young Mexican immigrants coming into the United States, the same is true for the majority of retirees who feel driven out of their own country.

The increasing cost of health care, an uncertain future for the Social Security system and a cost of living that keeps rising are a few of the factors that compel U.S. retirees to look beyond our borders for where they might spend their golden years.

Syndicated finance expert Scott Burns predicts that thousands more baby boomers will be crossing the U.S.-Mexico border in years to come just to sustain a lifestyle that will be harder to manage once they find themselves on fixed incomes.

Burns estimates, based on a range of data, that a retired couple living off $26,400 a year in Social Security benefits can raise their standard of living, without paying Medicare expenses, to $42,400 by moving to Mexico, where the cost of living can be up to 40% lower than in the USA.

Taking Advantage of Mexico's Welfare System

U.S. retirees who can't afford private Mexican health insurance can qualify for the Mexican Social Security system. Mexico's health care system charges only $270 annual premiums that include access to hospitals, outpatient clinics, and all medications and care at no additional costs.

It's no wonder that new retirement communities are sprouting up in Mexico, many in resort areas where lower property values and taxes help U.S. seniors stretch their retirement funds.

The nonprofit Migration Policy Institute reported in 2006 that from 1990 until 2000, several Mexican municipalities experienced high population growth fueled by this American influx: Chapala, 581% or 2,907 people; Mexicali, 117% or 1,446 people; Los Cabos, 308% or 709 people.

With all the fuss about how Mexican immigrants are changing the face of American society, it's interesting to note that the same is true in pockets of Mexico from American emigrants.

In those areas where U.S. retirees have flocked, English dominates and stores and businesses cater to American tastes and traditions—while in the heart of local Mexican society.

Sound familiar?

In a research report titled "America's Emigrants: U.S. Retirement Migration to Mexico and Panama," the authors found that few of the retirees are even fluent in Spanish, and while they bring more money into the local economy, they adversely impact it in other ways as well.

For instance, a Pan American Health Organization study found that many of the retirees suffer from diabetes, hypertension and heart disease—the costliest diseases to treat under the low-priced Mexican healthcare system.

Pricing Natives Out of Community

Also, because of the influx of American emigrants in some areas of the country, real estate is often priced out of reach of local Mexican citizens.

Sheila Croucher, professor of political science at Ohio's Miami University and the author of the upcoming University of Texas title *On the Other Side of the Fence: American Immigrants in Mexico*, further uncovered just how much U.S. emigrants are impacting our neighbors to the south.

In a conversation with officials from San Miguel de Allende, Croucher was told that U.S. citizens make up approximately 8–12,000 of the town's population of 80,000. But even that small percentage is enough to alter the economy in such a way that locals cannot afford to live in the heart of the city but are forced to move to the outskirts.

And when it comes to the issue of illegally working, some American emigrants are as guilty as their Mexican counterparts in the USA.

Though numbers are not precisely known, Mexican authorities know that there are some American emigrants who are working in Mexico without the proper paperwork and are not paying taxes.

San Miguel de Allende city officials have said that unlicensed businesses owned by foreigners cost the local government more than $360,000 a year in lost taxes and fees.

Croucher also found that while American emigrants have set up house in Mexico, they have not entirely separated themselves from the politics back home.

She calls this phenomenon "extra-territorial citizenship." In this age of cell phones, the Internet and globalization, the notion that citizenship extends beyond the confines of a specific territory is a progressive reality.

Regardless of which side of the border one comes from, this phenomenon is true and it just adds to the complexity of today's immigration issue.

Yet, it just goes to show that the immigration conversation is two-sided and ongoing. Each side has its share of the good and the bad, but the flow of people back and forth ultimately is good for both countries.

Mexico seems to understand this reality and is taking an open-minded approach.

Isn't it time we did, too?

Periodical Bibliography

The following articles have been selected to supplement the diverse views presented in this chapter.

Randal C. Archibold — "In Border Violence, Perception Is Greater than Crime Statistics," *New York Times*, June 20, 2010.

Charles Bowden — "Our Wall," *National Geographic*, May 2007.

Arian Campo-Flores — "Don't Fence Them In," *Newsweek*, June 7, 2010.

Eve Conant et al. — "The Enemy Within," *Newsweek*, March 23, 2009.

Duncan Currie — "The War Next Door," *National Review*, July 9, 2010.

Miriam Jordan — "Latest Immigration Wave: Retreat," *Wall Street Journal*, October 2, 2008.

Helmut Langerbein — "Great Blunders?: The Great Wall of China, the Berlin Wall, and the Proposed United States/Mexico Border Fence," *History Teacher*, November 2009.

Ruben Navarrette — "Allies in a Border War," *USA Today*, March 31, 2009.

Eva Sanchis — "Recession Hits Home, from Abroad," *World Policy Journal*, Spring 2009.

David Von Drehle — "A New Line in the Sand," *Time*, June 30, 2008.

OPPOSING
VIEWPOINTS®
SERIES

CHAPTER 4

What Should US Policy Be Toward Mexico?

Chapter Preface

When Mexican president Felipe Calderón took office in December 2006, he swiftly launched a military campaign to quell the violence between his country's feuding drug cartels. Some US lawmakers were impressed by Calderón's ability to put policy into action and his commitment to solving a problem that some Americans feared was spreading across the US-Mexican border. Calderón spoke about combating the drug problem and its resultant violence, however, as a responsibility shared by both the United States and Mexico. Wishing to support a leader who confronted the drug lords head-on, the George W. Bush administration proposed legislation to bolster Mexico's fighting capabilities.

Passed by Congress in 2008, the Mérida Initiative called for the release of $1.4 billion in aid to Mexican law enforcement over a three-year period. Other funds were earmarked to aid the police and military forces in other Latin American countries as part of the same initiative. Since President Barack Obama took office, another $300 million has been added to that total. One of the provisions of the initiative stipulates that the funds will not be released to the Mexican government; they go only to military and police organizations. In addition, the money has been spent primarily in the United States, purchasing helicopters and equipment that are sent to the appropriate Mexican agencies. Some funds have also been used to hire tacticians to train Mexican antidrug forces in the latest equipment and strategies.

In the chapter that follows, Armand Peschard-Sverdrup, a senior associate at the Center for Strategic and International Studies, insists the Mérida Initiative should command the full support of US lawmakers. "This initiative focuses on the future and on building the Mexican government's capacity to make sure that potential threats are stopped in Mexico well before they reach US borders or communities," Peschard-Sverdrup asserts. Supporters like Peschard-Sverdrup claim that only by building up Mexico's fighting capacity can the drug cartels be controlled. Critics of the plan, though, contend that no amount of helicopters or sophisticated police equipment can end this problem. In a May 2008 review for the Woodrow Wilson International Center for Scholars, Andrew Selee made the point that "the consumption of narcotics in the United States remains high and continues to grow in Mexico, and no law enforcement strategy against drug trafficking will be successful without significantly lowering demand." Some also worry that building up the military and paramilitary police forces has led to a rise in human rights violations in regions where these units are deployed.

President Calderón has tried to ease concerns detractors have about the Mérida Initiative. He has vowed to reduce military presence by recruiting more police officers who can handle the antidrug assignments, and he agreed to more transparency in state court trials against those accused of drug crimes. In response, the Obama administration has been pushing for Mérida II, a new policy to take over when the initial plan terminates. This outgrowth of the first Mérida Initiative will focus less on buttressing police efforts and more on aiding governmental and judicial reforms. It will also attempt to streamline information sharing between the two countries in the ongoing fight against drug trafficking. Skeptics and advocates of the new plan abound, but as Council on Foreign Relations researcher Dora Beszterczey writes in a March 29, 2010, entry for the *Americas Quarterly* blog, "Beyond the lofty rhetoric, tangible results are a long way off and both sides of the partnership will need to demonstrate sustained focus and real commitments to maintain today's positive tone underlying the partnership."

The Mérida Initiative is just one aspect of US policy toward Mexico examined in the following chapter. Other experts whose views are provided in this chapter offer varying proposals on how the United States can help Mexico fight violence and corruption while not sacrificing America's own security.

> "The Mexican border could and should
> be made a permanent duty station for
> U.S. troops."

The United States Should Militarize the Border

Dave Gibson

In the viewpoint that follows, Dave Gibson insists that the United States should position military units along the border with Mexico to stem the tide of drug smugglers and illegal immigrants. He maintains that the Mexican drug cartels employ military and paramilitary forces to protect smugglers crossing the border, therefore the US government should meet this threat with equal force. In Gibson's view, the country has the manpower to militarize the border region; it only lacks the political will to put such a plan in place. Gibson is a former senatorial aid who currently works as a writer. He believes immigration is the most pressing issue for the United States to address and manage.

As you read, consider the following questions:

1. From where does Gibson say the United States should draw the thirty thousand combat troops he believes are necessary to secure the US-Mexican border?

2. Since 1996, how many times has the Mexican military crossed the border into the United States, as Gibson reports?

3. According to a 2009 Justice Department report cited by the author, in how many US cities have Mexican drug cartels set up operations?

In 2005, the [President George W.] Bush administration used U.S. combat troops to patrol the borders which define Iraq. In fact, at the time, he announced that there would be a complete lockdown on Iraq's borders during that nation's elections. [President Barack] Obama is now using our troops in that same capacity, as well as in providing border security for Afghanistan.

While protecting the borders of foreign lands has been a priority for both Presidents Bush and Obama, neither has ever shown a portion of that commitment to their own country.

Send in Troops Now

Rather than sending a few hundred National Guardsmen to the nearly 2,000-mile-long border, functioning under orders to step aside when confronted with those who cross our border illegally (even when they are armed drug smugglers), the way Bush did, we should send 30,000 troops to the U.S./ Mexican border immediately.

If that number of troops—along with their tanks, helicopters, and U.S. Air Force overflights—were utilized along the border, illegal entries would come to a sudden, screeching halt.

Where would the personnel come from?

We could simply take the troops from Germany, where 30,000 of our troops are stationed, or from South Korea, where a similar number now work for the protection of the Korean peninsula, rather than for that of the American Southwest.

Between Iraq and Afghanistan, we now have about 200,000 troops deployed, with many of those soldiers on their fourth and fifth tours of duty. Despite the death of 5,300 U.S. soldiers, any reasonable American would be hard-pressed to explain the achieved benefits to this nation, in either of those two countries.

Conversely, the benefits from using our military to defend our border with Mexico would be immediately visible, particularly by this country's police officers.

Mexican Soldiers Routinely Cross the Border

Units of the Mexican military regularly cross the border into this country. The well-armed units escort drug and human smugglers and even fire upon U.S. Border Patrol agents. It is estimated that Latin American drug cartels spend more than $500 million annually, paying off high-ranking Mexican military and police officials.

Former Congressman Tom Tancredo (R-CO) said in a 2002 interview: "There's no doubt Mexican military units along the border are being controlled by drug cartels, and not by Mexico City. The military units operate freely, with little or no direction, and several of them have made numerous incursions into the United States."

In January 2008, the Department of Homeland Security reported that since 1996, there had been 278 known incursions by the Mexican military into the United States. They are often seen providing armed escort to drug smugglers. Incredibly, the Mexican military now enters our nation at will, with no response from the U.S. government.

Illegal aliens account for 29 percent of our total prison population. Many more Mexican criminals still roam our streets. The 18th Street Gang [set up in Los Angeles by Mexican American youth], and MS-13 [a gang set up in Los Angeles by Salvadoran immigrants] have already taken over the streets of Los Angeles, now they are staking out territory across the country. One million Mexican criminals is equivalent to 50 divisions of enemy soldiers within this country.

Meeting the Threat Head-On

U.S. Attorney General Eric Holder has stated: "International drug trafficking organizations pose a sustained, serious threat to the safety and security of our communities. We can provide our communities the safety and the security that they deserve only by confronting these dangerous cartels head-on without reservation."

Holder's statement was made during a press conference following a February 2009 nationwide raid which netted 750 drug cartel operatives.

A 2009 Justice Department report identified 231 U.S. cities in which the cartels now operate. The list stretches from Tucson, AZ (Federation, Juárez) to Buffalo, NY (Gulf).

While it is not surprising that drug cartel activity is occurring in American cities close to the largely unprotected U.S.-Mexican border, it may be shocking to some that the Atlanta, GA, area has become the site of major operations for the drug cartels.

According to the Justice Department's National Drug Intelligence Center, more than one cartel has adopted Atlanta as their principal distribution center for the East Coast.

During 2008, the Drug Enforcement Administration seized $70 million in cash in Atlanta, which surpassed every other U.S. region. By March, over $30 million had been seized in Atlanta for 2009, as compared to $19 million in Los Angeles, and $18 million in Chicago.

Jack Killorin, head of the Office of National Drug Control Policy's federal task force in Atlanta, recently told *USA Today*: "The same folks who are rolling heads in the streets of Ciudad Juárez are operating in Atlanta."

The Mexican border could and should be made a permanent duty station for U.S. troops. This would allow the Border Patrol to fully staff the official entry points, which would dramatically reduce the amount of drugs and number of criminals coming into this country through those checkpoints on a daily basis.

We have the resources to defend this nation, we need only the political will to do so.

"*Talk about sending U.S. combat troops to Mexico is crazy.*"

The United States Should Not Send Troops into Mexico

Andres Oppenheimer

Pulitzer Prize–winning journalist Andres Oppenheimer is a columnist for the Miami Herald. *He is the author of several books including* Saving the Americas: The Dangerous Decline of Latin America and What the U.S. Must Do. *In the following viewpoint, Oppenheimer rejects calls to deploy US military troops to Mexico to stem the drug trade and the violence that surrounds it. In his opinion, the military would only increase tensions between the two countries and lead to civil strife at home. Oppenheimer believes the US government should expand cooperative efforts with Mexico to make headway against the drug cartels.*

As you read, consider the following questions:

1. According to Oppenheimer, which Arizona sheriff boasts of his record of putting forty thousand illegal aliens in jail?

2. As Oppenheimer relates, what does Mexican ambassador Arturo Sarukhan think the United States should do to help stem the power of the drug cartels?

3. How does the author think the US government should utilize the military to combat the drug trade and border violence?

The escalation of drug-related violence in Mexico—including the mass execution of 72 migrants last week [in August 2010]—is moving a small but growing number of U.S. foreign policy hawks to call for a radical solution: Send in the U.S. Army.

I'm not kidding. At first, I thought it was a joke, or the kind of overreaction that is most often confined to the blogosphere.

But, increasingly, populist local U.S. officials are seriously talking about sending in U.S. troops to end the drug-related violence that has cost 28,000 lives in Mexico over the past four years, and that occasionally spills over to the U.S. side of the border.

The U.S. military would help crack down on the drug cartels, and help stop illegal immigration and terrorism, they claim. President Barack Obama's recent decision to deploy up to 1,200 National Guard troops along the southwest border with Mexico has obviously not pacified them.

When I interviewed Sheriff Joe Arpaio of four million-population Maricopa County, Arizona, about his hard-line immigration views last week, I was ready to hear a lot of tough talk against undocumented immigrants, but I wasn't expecting him to advocate sending U.S. troops to Mexico.

Views from Both Sides of the Issue

Arpaio, a darling of conservative talk shows who prides himself on having put 40,000 undocumented migrants behind bars and promotes himself as "America's toughest sheriff," lashed out against Mexican laws that prohibit U.S. troops from engaging in battle inside Mexico. During his years as a Drug Enforcement Administration agent in Mexico, he actively fought against the drug cartels, he said.

"When I was a director there, my agents worked undercover. They were involved in gun battles. They worked with the military, they worked with the federales [police]. . . . We were operational, approved by the Mexican government," Arpaio said. "Why don't we do the same right now?"

"I'm not a proponent of the Army of the United States being involved in law enforcement, but we have armies right now in Afghanistan, Iraq. . . . We go into other countries. Why can't we go into Mexico with their cooperation?" he asked. Asked to elaborate, he said it would have to be done with Mexico's approval.

Mexico's ambassador to the United States, Arturo Sarukhan, told me that sending U.S. troops to Mexico "is a nonstarter." Another Mexican official told me that Mexicans are very sensitive about the U.S. military interventions that resulted in the annexation of Texas and California in the 1830s and 1840s, and that the presence of U.S. combat troops in the country would be politically explosive.

"The United States can continue to play a constructive role by stepping up efforts to stop the flow of U.S. small arms to Mexico—80 percent of all successfully traced weapons in Mexico come from the United States—and speed up disbursement of $1.4 billion in law enforcement equipment under the Mérida Initiative," Sarukhan said.

What the United States Should Do Instead of Sending in Troops

My opinion: Talk about sending U.S. combat troops to Mexico is crazy. You would have anti-U.S. student demonstrations starting a day later, followed by a dead protester who would immediately become a national and international martyr, followed by resurgence of leftist guerrillas, followed by a cycle of violence that would lead to more bloodshed than the current war on the drug cartels.

What should Washington do, then? First, take a deep breath and think calmly. Mexico's murder rate is rising fast, but as we reported in this column on March 24, according to United Nations figures it's still about five times less than that of Honduras, Jamaica, or Venezuela, and significantly less than that of Washington, D.C. The United States should not overreact.

Second, it would be a good idea for both Mexico and the United States to significantly increase their military forces on their respective borders: in Mexico's case, to stop the drug flow, and in the U.S. case, to stop the arms and money smuggling.

And third, it's time to start thinking about a significant expansion of the U.S. Mérida Initiative [aimed at curbing the cross-border drug trade through cooperation between Mexico and the United States].

Washington should provide Mexico with more helicopters, intelligence and—above all—technical assistance and training to create police academies that would help dismantle Mexico's 2,200 corruption-ridden police forces, and replace them with more reliable ones. Everything, except sending U.S. troops.

| "[The Mérida Initiative] makes strategic
| sense for the United States, and it is
| also sound public policy."

US Lawmakers Should Support the Mérida Initiative

Armand Peschard-Sverdrup

The Mérida Initiative is cooperative security legislation between the United States, Mexico, and Central American nations. It was signed into law on June 30, 2008, and its chief aim is to help Mexico strengthen its law enforcement through training and technology sharing with US counterparts. The United States intends to release $400 million in aid contracts to Mexico to provide helicopters and other progressive technologies to combat the growing drug cartels that have perpetrated violence along the US-Mexican border and throughout other parts of the nation. In the following viewpoint, written a few months before the initiative passed Congress, Armand Peschard-Sverdrup urges US legislators to support this initiative. He attests that the Mexican government has shown a willingness to take on the cartels, and he expects the cooperative venture will help both the United States and Mexico curb drug trafficking and gun trade. Peschard-

Armand Peschard-Sverdrup, "Five Perspectives on the Mérida Initiative: What It Is and Why It Must Succeed," Latin American Outlook, no. 1, March 2008. AEI.com. Copyright © 2008 by American Enterprise Institute. Reproduced by permission.

Sverdrup is the chief executive officer of Peschard-Sverdrup & Associates, a consulting firm that helps companies do business in Mexico. He is also a senior associate at the Center for Strategic and International Studies.

As you read, consider the following questions:

1. According to the author, under the jurisdiction of what ministry does Felipe Calderón intend to unify Mexico's law enforcement?

2. Why does Peschard-Sverdrup believe Mexican lawmakers will not perceive the Mérida Initiative as an example of the US government intruding on Mexican sovereignty?

3. Why does the author claim that US lawmakers should ignore short-term electoral concerns and authorize the Mérida Initiative quickly?

An accurate assessment of the Mérida Initiative should take into account several aspects that may be misunderstood or overlooked, especially in light of the need to get the support and level of funding from a U.S. Congress that is weary of the unending demand for U.S. aid—not to mention at a time when the U.S. economy seems to be entering a recession and especially in an election year.

Building Up Mexico's Law Enforcement

The Mérida Initiative is designed to strengthen a wide range of Mexico's security-oriented institutions—such as the Secretariat of Public Security, the Office of the Attorney General, Mexican Customs, and the National Institute of Migration—and to professionalize the country's law enforcement personnel. The U.S. Congress runs the risk of getting it wrong if members assume that the initiative deals simply with today's problems and is solely a counternarcotics measure. This initiative focuses on the future and on building the Mexican government's capacity to make sure that potential threats are stopped in Mexico well before they reach U.S. borders or communities. If the U.S. Congress and the American people do not look at the program in this way, precious time will be lost; strengthening institutions does not take place overnight. The initiative will ultimately help ensure the collective security of both nations against future threats.

The [Felipe] Calderón administration's demonstrated commitment to combating organized crime during its first year in office provides an opportunity for the United States to engage our neighbor in a way that will collectively ensure the future security of both nations. Quite frankly, the priority that the Mexican government has placed on shoring up its security institutions is not new—it is not even an effort that the Calderón administration initiated. In fact, former president Ernesto Zedillo, together with the Mexican Congress, implemented some of the reforms needed for this effort back in the mid-1990s when they created the Deputy Ministry of Public Security and enacted an initial round of judicial reforms. Former president Vicente Fox and the Mexican Congress followed through by implementing additional reforms designed to protect national and public security, among them converting the Deputy Ministry of Public Security into a stand-alone ministry. Calderón has demonstrated his interest in building on his predecessors' accomplishments by integrating the various federal law enforcement agencies under the unified command and control of the Ministry of Public Security and strengthening the prosecutorial capacity of the Office of the Attorney General. Both measures are aimed at rendering the federal government more effective in combating crime and obtaining indictments, thus strengthening Mexico's culture of rule of law.

One must bear in mind that Mexico is still undergoing its own process of democratic consolidation. Mexico has always enjoyed a very strong executive branch; since 1997, when the Mexican Congress started to become more pluralistic, the legislative branch gradually gained more autonomy and today exhibits true separation of powers. The judiciary is still, relatively speaking, the weakest of Mexico's three branches of government. Over and above the security it gives to both nations, this initiative provides valuable support to a neighbor that is committed to strengthening the government's judiciary and thus its rule of law.

Mérida Is an Ongoing Partnership, Not a Quick Solution

The perception that the United States is encroaching on Mexican sovereignty has always been the Achilles' heel of conceptualizing any type of bilateral program, so we must be respectful of Mexico's sensitivities. The Mérida Initiative is far from an encroachment on Mexican sovereignty. In fact, it is fully consistent with Calderón's agenda and therefore should provide additional impetus for him to implement many of the administration's objectives laid out in his National Development Plan for 2006–2012. This initiative is also consistent with the goals set by the Mexican Congress, which approved a 24 percent spending increase in 2007 for security agencies over the amount appropriated in fiscal year 2006. Consequently, it makes perfect sense for the United States to assist Mexico in acquiring the skill sets and technology that are interoperable with those of U.S. agencies so that Mexico can participate in joint operations against common enemies and enhance both countries' national security. Regardless of what may have occurred in the past, both nations must be vigilant and remain aware of future security threats, and that calls for a much closer collaborative relationship between U.S. and Mexican security agencies.

Both countries must recognize that the Mérida Initiative is not a silver bullet. It would be a mistake to think that $1.4 billion will solve Mexico's security problems overnight or that

US Commitment to Equipment and Training

As of March 31, 2010, the United States had made several deliveries of equipment and training in Mexico and Central America under the Mérida Initiative. The United States has delivered items including five Bell helicopters, biometric equipment, immigration computer equipment and software, forensics lab equipment, and canines to Mexico.... In addition, the United States has assisted in training over 4,000 police graduates from Mexico's federal police training facility, the academy at San Luis Potosí. In Central America, the United States has provided over 60 contraband detection kits, police vehicles, and training.

US Government Accountability Office,
"Mérida Initiative: The United States Has Provided
Counternarcotics and Anticrime Support
but Needs Better Performance Measures,"
Report to Congressional Requesters, July 2010.

it will achieve the results that are likely to be promised as the initiative makes its way through the U.S. legislative process. It is true that investing in noninvasive technology can help shore up the integrity of cargo entering and exiting both nations. The technology, however, has to be operational, it has to be well positioned, and problems with it have to be acted on by officials in each nation. In addition, investing in the professionalization of law enforcement agencies will yield the needed results only if Mexico is successful in recruiting the type of individuals who are genuinely interested in an honorable career in law enforcement as opposed to merely seeing the job as a means to illicit enrichment.

Saving Mérida from Party Politics

All nations, including Mexico, aspire to provide their citizens the quality of life that comes from possessing a culture of rule of law. Calderón has not only diagnosed the problem of insecurity and impunity accurately, but also—and more importantly—demonstrated the political will to implement the various judicial and security-oriented reforms that are required to meet these goals.

Some major institutional restructuring that has taken place in the United States—from the creation of the Department of Defense in 1947 to the creation of the Department of Homeland Security in 2003—was prompted by compelling events: World War II or the terrorist attacks of September 11 [2001], for example. Mexico has yet to experience an event of this magnitude. But Mexico's political leaders, regardless of their party affiliation, are fully aware that they need to push through a sweeping reorganization of Mexico's judiciary and law enforcement apparatus. The Mérida Initiative has the potential to serve as a tipping point for needed judicial and security-oriented reforms.

As the Mérida Initiative is debated in the U.S. Congress, many things are likely to be said, and some grandstanding may take place, particularly during an election year. It is important that the Mexican people realize that this tug-of-war is a natural part of the relationship between the executive and legislative branches of government and is needed to maintain a system of checks and balances. The U.S. Congress will demand that the [President George W.] Bush administration makes sure that U.S. monies are well spent. Even though talk of conditionality will inevitably cause some in Mexico to complain, "We told you so—here are the imperialists telling us what we should be doing," it is to be hoped that such voices will be in the minority. After all, the Mexican people now have a much more mature relationship between their executive and legislative branches and have acquired an appreciation for the type of debate that will revolve around this initiative.

It is a matter of concern, however, that the Mérida Initiative could fall victim to campaign strategists who see it, along with immigration and U.S.-Mexican border security, as an effective wedge issue as their candidates head into the 2008 presidential and congressional elections—an issue aimed at polarizing the U.S. electorate both between Republicans and Democrats and within each party. This would clearly be the case if the measure were to fail to win congressional approval in the first quarter. One would hope that members of Congress will recognize that the strategic long-term gains to be realized from the initiative far outweigh the short-term electoral gains that could conceivably be achieved among certain segments of the electorate. If Calderón's interest in the Mérida Initiative were to go unanswered, it would take a considerable amount of time to recreate the conditions necessary for the unprecedented level of cooperation that is called for in the Mérida Initiative. The opportunity is there, and failure to approve the program would mark a setback in U.S.-Mexican cooperation at a time when working together is of vital importance for the future security of both nations.

The Mérida Initiative is neither a Republican nor a Democratic issue. It is an initiative that makes strategic sense for the United States, and it is also sound public policy. In fact, the Mérida Initiative builds on many of the U.S.-Mexican bilateral accomplishments of presidents George H.W. Bush and Bill Clinton—and the respective U.S. Congresses during those administrations—and is a natural next step for the current president and Congress.

I "*Militarization is not the way to deal with Mexico's political crisis.*"

US Lawmakers Should Abandon the Mérida Initiative

Laura Carlsen

In the following viewpoint, Laura Carlsen argues that the Mérida Initiative, an agreement between the United States, Mexico, and Central American countries, should be halted. Carlsen claims the initiative—which seeks to curb drug trafficking through aid to Mexico's security and law enforcement organizations—does not have the concerns of Mexico at heart. She insists that the expansion of a "war on drugs" program is flawed, given that the model has already failed, in her opinion, in the United States. She believes building up Mexico's security forces has only led to more deaths and human rights abuses in areas where these forces are deployed. Carlsen advocates that Congress end the Mérida plan and focus aid to alleviate the root causes of the growing drug trade, such as poverty, unemployment, and inequality. Carlsen is the director of the Mexico City–based Americas Program of the Center for International Policy and a writer whose work has appeared in numerous news and research venues.

Laura Carlsen, "Perils of Plan Mexico: Going Beyond Security to Strengthen U.S.-Mexico Relations," Americas Program, November 23, 2009. CIPAmericas.org. Copyright © 2009 by CIP Americas. Reproduced by permission.

As you read, consider the following questions:

1. According to Carlsen, in what trade agreement does the Mérida Initiative have its roots?

2. In Carlsen's view, who was unjustly targeted by President Calderón's Joint Operation Chihuahua?

3. As the author reports, the Mérida Initiative includes a provision to withhold some of the aid money pending Mexico's proof of progress in what area?

Mexico is the United States' closest Latin American neighbor and yet most U.S. citizens receive little reliable information about what is happening within the country. Instead, Mexico and Mexicans are often demonized in the U.S. press. The single biggest reason for this is the way that the entire binational relationship has been recast in terms of security over the past few years.

From a neighbor and a trade partner, Mexico has been portrayed as a threat to U.S. national security. Immigrants are no longer immigrants, but criminals, "removable aliens," and even potential terrorists. Latinos, mostly Mexicans, are now the largest group of victims of hate crimes in the United States.

Although Mexico-bashing has been a favorite sport of the right for years, this terrible conversion of Mexico, from an ally to a "failed state" and narco-haven in the media and policy circles, began in earnest under the [President George W.] Bush administration and has only intensified since then. The Mérida Initiative and the militarization of Mexico are the direct outgrowth of the national security framework imposed on bilateral relations.

The Motivation for Mérida

There is a misconception that the Mérida Initiative, named after a meeting between Presidents [Felipe] Calderón and Bush in the city of Mérida, originated when Calderón requested assistance in the drug war from the U.S. government. The U.S. government, this story goes, agreed to comply. When the U.S. government cited its share of responsibility in the transnational drug trade as the world's largest market, pundits heralded the admission as unprecedented and a new step in binational cooperation.

This is largely myth. In fact, Plan Mexico—as it was first called—has its roots in the Security and Prosperity Partnership [of North America (SPP)] that grew out of the North American Free Trade Agreement [NAFTA]. When the regional trade agreement was expanded into a security agreement, the Bush administration sought a means to extend its national security doctrine to its regional trade partners. This meant that both Canada and Mexico were to assume counterterrorism activities (despite the absence of international terrorism threats in those nations), border security (in Mexico's case, to control Central American migrants), and protection of strategic resources and investments. Assistant Secretary of State Tom Shannon called it "arming NAFTA."

The Bush announcement of the three-year Mérida Initiative in October of 2007 extended U.S. military intervention in Mexico from this base. The plan is dubbed a "counterterrorism, counter-narcotics, and border security initiative," although it's the war on drugs that has received the most attention. Although U.S. troops cannot operate by law in Mexican territory, the plan significantly increases the presence of U.S. agents and intelligence services, now estimated at 1,400, and of U.S. private security companies throughout Mexico.

The terms of the Mérida Initiative send the full $1.3 billion appropriated so far to U.S. defense, security, information technology and other private-sector firms, and the U.S. government. One hundred percent of the money stays in the United States since the plan prohibits cash payments to Mexico.

In other words, what it does is ensure an expanding market for defense and security contracts, in an undeclared war that has no exit strategy in sight.

Does this sound familiar?

Calderón Legitimizes His Presidency with a War on Drugs

It's important to note that despite obvious threats to Mexican sovereignty, the Calderón government lobbied actively for the Mérida Initiative, balking only at certain human rights conditions. There is a reason for Calderón's enthusiasm, which has to do with this particular moment in Mexico's fragile democracy.

Recall that Felipe Calderón took office after courts proclaimed he had won the elections by half a percentage point. The courts blocked a demand for a full recount, despite evidence of irregularities and the narrow margin. The election decision enraged an already divided populace and failed to resolve accusations of fraud.

The military had enabled Calderón to take office by physically escorting him into a Congress occupied by protestors and placing the presidential banner over his shoulder. The country was in the throes of massive protests involving at least half the populace.

Once in office, Calderón launched the war on drugs. This strategy allowed a weak president with little popular legitimacy to cement his power, based on building an alliance with the armed forces under a militarized counter-narcotics model.

The war on drugs model created an external enemy to distract from the internal protests and division. With its focus on interdiction and supply-side enforcement, the model was originally developed by President Richard Nixon in the '70s to increase presidential power, by taking counter-narcotics efforts out of the hands of communities, where it was treated largely as a community health issue, and placing it in the hands of the executive, where it was treated as a security issue.

Applied in Mexico, the immediate effect was to send more than 45,000 army troops into Mexican communities. The presence of the army in all aspects of public security is now the major cause of the grave increase in human rights violations and drug-related violence in Mexico.

The militarization of Mexico has led to a steep increase in homicides related to the drug war. It has led to rape and abuse of women by soldiers in communities throughout the country. Human rights complaints against the armed forces have increased sixfold.

Even these stark figures do not reflect the seriousness of what is happening in Mexican society. Many abuses are not reported at all for the simple reason that there is no assurance that justice will be done. The Mexican Armed Forces are not subject to civilian justice systems, but to their own military tribunals. These very rarely terminate in convictions. Of scores of reported torture cases, for example, not a single case has been prosecuted by the army in recent years.

The situation with the police and civilian court system is not much better. Corruption is rampant due to the immense economic power of the drug cartels. Local and state police, the political system, and the justice system are so highly infiltrated and controlled by the cartels that in most cases it is impossible to tell the good guys from the bad guys.

Stifling Dissent

The militarization of Mexico has also led to what rights groups call "the criminalization of protest." Peasant and indigenous leaders have been framed under drug charges and communities harassed by the military with the pretext of the drug war. In [Joint] Operation Chihuahua, one of the first military operations to replace local police forces and occupy whole towns, among the first people picked up were grassroots leaders—not on drug charges but on three-year-old warrants for leading anti-NAFTA protests. Recently, grassroots organizations opposing transnational mining operations in the Sierra Madre cited a sharp increase in militarization that they link to the Mérida Initiative and the NAFTA-SPP aimed at opening up natural resources to transnational investment.

All this—the human rights abuses, impunity, corruption, criminalization of the opposition—would be grave cause for concern under any conditions. What is truly incomprehensible is that in addition to generating these costs to Mexican society, the war on drugs doesn't work to achieve its own stated objectives.

We know this not only from the relatively recent Mexican experience, but from other places—especially Colombia and the Andean region. As Plan Colombia goes into its tenth year, the cost of drugs on U.S. streets has gone down and regional production has risen. In Mexico, interdictions dropped between 2007 and 2008. The number of arrests went up but seems to have little effect on the hydra-headed cartels. Actual indictment and prosecution rates following arrests are suspiciously not reported. Illegal-drug flows to the U.S. market appear to be unaffected overall.

Ending the "War on Drugs" Model

To understand the U.S. role in this mess, it's necessary to step back a moment. There is no question that the power of organized crime in Mexico is real. There is also no question that the current approach to combating it is a disaster in its effects on human rights and democracy, and a quagmire in strategic terms.

In this context, the question is why, particularly now that George Bush is out of office, would the U.S. government continue to concentrate its aid to Mexico in a way that demonstrably empowers corrupt security forces, violates Mexican hu-

Reinforcing a War-Like Mentality

The most severe flaw in the Mérida Initiative is that it reinforces the war-like mentality that has led Mexico to deploy its military and police in a territorial battle against criminals as the answer to drug trafficking. This war on crime has brought with it a steeply escalating universe of human rights violations against Mexico's residents, including arbitrary killings, torture, and illegal arrests. Furthermore, this strategy has not led to a decrease in drug-related violence but rather has seen a tripling of drug-related homicides in the past three years, with the number of killings in 2008 now estimated at 5,630 and with more than 1,000 killings reported by Mexican media for the first fifty-one days of 2009.

Stephanie Erin Brewer,
"Rethinking the Mérida Initiative: Why the U.S. Must
Change Course in Its Approach to Mexico's Drug War,"
Human Rights Brief, American University Washington
College of Law Center for Human Rights
and Humanitarian Law, Spring 2009.

man rights, and leads to an increase in violence? This is a huge mistake with extremely high costs.

At a time when Mexico faces one of its worst economic crises in history, U.S. foreign policy toward our neighbor to the south reduces one of our most important and complex bilateral relations to miscast and failed security cooperation under a discredited war on drugs model. We know that there are powerful economic and political interests behind creating a war front in Mexico. But we also know that we too can have a powerful voice. The question is how?

Many U.S. citizen groups have been grappling with that issue. The effort to place human rights conditions on the military police aid package to Mexico turned out to be counter-productive. The original conditions withheld 15% of some Mérida Initiative aid pending progress on the prohibition against torture—a common practice by Mexican security forces to punish community leaders and extract confessions—consultation with human rights groups, transparency, and committing the army to civilian courts where permitted under law. None of that happened in a real way.

Nevertheless, the State Department recently sent a human rights report to Congress showing that the Mexican government had not made significant progress on conditions, while asking Congress to release the funds on the basis of good intentions. Congress promptly complied.

For this reason, our organization [the Americas Program] and many other U.S. and Mexican groups are calling for a halt to Plan Mexico as the three-year cycle closes. The [President Barack] Obama administration has pledged to continue military funding to Mexico and Central America under the plan, but we believe that a thorough analysis of the results and consequences will demonstrate the need for a more integral and effective aid strategy and help us chart a binational relationship focused on peaceful cooperation and community building.

We are not alone in demanding that the war on drugs model be replaced.

In Mexico, recent polls show that the majority of the population has lost faith in the drug war model. Last May [2009], 52 Mexican human rights organizations called for an end to military aid to their government under the Mérida Initiative. Their letter reads:

"We respectfully request that the U.S. Congress and Department of State, in both the Mérida Initiative as in other programs to support public security in Mexico, does not allocate funds or direct programs to the armed forces. . . .

"We urge the United States to consider ways to support a holistic response to security problems; based on tackling the root causes of violence and ensuring the full respect of human rights; not on the logic of combat."

Redirecting America's Aid to Mexico

In the United States, the AFL-CIO [American Federation of Labor-Congress of Industrial Organizations] has come out against the Mérida Initiative, in part as a protest against the violation of labor rights particularly in the case of the mining union but also as a rejection of the drug war model. U.S. labor took this position even before Calderón used the army last week to wipe out Mexico's oldest union and throw 45,000 unionized workers out overnight. The drug war facilitated the use of the army to take over the state-owned company's installations.

The 1.7-million-person Labor Council for Latin American Advancement; nongovernmental organizations including CIP [Center for International Policy], Americas Program and Global Exchange; religious organizations including Witness for Peace, the Maryknoll Office for Global Concerns, and Tikkun [Ministries]; and grassroots activist organizations like the Latin America Solidarity Coalition, Alliance for Democracy, the Committee in Solidarity with the People of El Salvador, and Friends of Brad Will have all called for U.S. citizens to oppose the plan and redirect aid to Mexico to health and development programs.

The immediate change needed is relatively simple, although the situation is not. The U.S. government should:

1. Understand shared responsibility in the transnational drug war not as intervention into Mexican security issues but as assuming its own responsibilities in reducing demand, increasing health services, and attacking cor-

ruption within its borders. Much public funding and political commitment is needed here, as well as a serious search for models to replace the failed drug war.

2. The U.S. government must rechannel harmful security aid to Mexico into development and anti-crisis aid that will address the root factors that have led to the expansion of drug consumption and trafficking in Mexico. Proposals for this type of aid have already been presented before Congress.

Militarization is not the way to deal with Mexico's political crisis and infusing government money into industries based on blood is not the way to deal with the U.S. economic crisis.

Mexico should be a U.S. priority. But providing exclusively security-focused equipment and training to Mexico is like pouring gas on a fire.

Citizens in both countries stand to lose by viewing the complex binational relationship through the reductionist lens of national security. Critical issues have fallen from the agenda or receive merely lip service. Among them: transborder livelihoods in the world's most integrated borderlands, immigration, regional environmental threats, trade, and a sustainable energy future.

We must return the U.S.-Mexico relationship to the simple equation that a healthy neighbor equals better trade, security, and cultural relations.

A strong and mutually beneficial relationship must cover the full range of issues between the two nations. The Obama administration and Congress must reorient the militarized relationship with Mexico. A new approach must go to the roots of the illegal drug trade by addressing inequality, poverty, employment, and the high costs of prohibitionist policies. Instead of seeking to bolster the Calderón administration, and police and military forces characterized by corruption, we must stand by human rights, democratic institutions, and a strong role for civil society.

> "*The U.S. should openly join the conversation on strategic and selective decriminalization of drugs like marijuana and impose strict controls on gun sales along the U.S. side of our common border.*"

The United States Should End the War on Drugs and Strictly Control Gun Sales

Ted Lewis

In the following viewpoint, Ted Lewis claims that the United States could help Mexico curb the violence surrounding the drug trade in that country by making two policy changes: legalizing marijuana and enacting stricter gun controls. In Lewis's opinion, these measures would reduce the demand for Mexican narcotics and deprive the cartels of their easy access to weapons. Lewis directs the Mexico Program of Global Exchange, an education and resource center that advocates a sustainable world and promotes workers' rights in an era of globalization.

As you read, consider the following questions:

1. According to the author, what percentage of the twenty-eight thousand slayings in Mexico since 2006 has been investigated by Mexican authorities?

2. In Lewis's view, why doesn't the United States enact a ban on assault rifle sales?

3. What percentage of the seventy-five thousand guns Mexican authorities seized from criminals since 2007 has come from the United States, as reported by the author?

For Mexico, 2010 is a deeply symbolic year. Mexicans celebrate 200 years of independence from Spain and the 100th anniversary of the Mexican Revolution. Their government will spend $300 million on the party, but no amount of fireworks or revolutionary nostalgia can overcome the inescapable sensation that Mexico is sinking into crisis.

Drug-gang assassins recently massacred 72 Central and South American migrants. The two local and state investigators who first arrived at the crime scene disappeared and were found dead two weeks later. Gunmen killed three Mexican mayors in the past month.

Mexico Out of Control

In the first four years of President Felipe Calderón's drug war, more than 28,000 people have been slain, according to the government's own count. Yet there have been few prosecutions: less than 5 percent of these murders have been investigated. But even those who are inured to corruption and incompetence are sickened by news of a prison warden who let a death squad out at night over a period of months—driving official vehicles and armed with prison guard assault rifles—to massacre innocent people in a neighboring state.

Headlines from Mexico bleed with news of such brutal killings and government ineptitude. And even as the violence continues to build, a recession—spreading south from the United States—cuts to the economic bones of an already vulnerable Mexican population. Growing economic desperation and shocking violence have undermined Mexicans' faith in the ability of their government to manage the economy, control the country's streets, mete out justice, or even to remain neutral among the warring cartels seeking to control North America's drug-trade corridors.

It sounds bad and thus it is tempting to turn our gaze away from the news of mayhem and sadistic acts of violence coming out of Mexico. But we must not, and cannot afford to, turn away. The well-being of Mexico is vital to the well-being of the United States. We are neighbors and economic partners who share a continent and a common destiny. Any effective prescription to pull Mexico back from the abyss will require cooperation—as well as introspection and substantive policy changes—from the United States.

Halting the Flow of Guns and Money to Drug Cartels

The U.S. should openly join the conversation on strategic and selective decriminalization of drugs like marijuana and impose strict controls on gun sales along the U.S. side of our common border. Clearly, most of Mexico's problems need to be solved in Mexico, by Mexicans, but these are two crucial steps we can take on our side of the border to reduce the flow of money and guns fueling Mexico's drug mafias. This one-two punch would deliver a damaging blow to the criminal organizations terrorizing Mexico.

A consensus is jelling on both sides of the border that it is time to move beyond the prohibitionist dogmas that have shaped—and doomed—the drug "war" since its declaration by [President] Richard Nixon in the early 1970s. In Mexico, a

"The Middleman: Drugs from Mexico, Guns from US," by Pletch—Eldon Pletcher. www.CartoonStock.com.

chorus of opinion leaders including former President Vicente Fox have forced open a long-pent-up debate on drug legalization. President Calderón recently made news by endorsing debate on this topic, even as he reassured Washington, D.C., of his own continued allegiance to the prohibition camp.

Americans are the prime customers for the narcotics produced in and shipped through Mexico. Despite 40 years and hundreds of billions of dollars spent on the drug war's eradication and interdiction plans, prohibited drugs are easily available across the United States today. Their illegality assures the inflated profits that sustain criminal organizations.

Legislation That Would Make a Difference

This fall [of 2010], Californians may pass a ballot measure to end marijuana prohibition. That would be an important step, but irrespective of California's choice, it is our federal drug and gun policies that must evolve to aid Mexicans fighting to preserve the soul of their country.

Mexicans often ask why the U.S. doesn't ban the assault weapons that can still be legally purchased on our side of the border. The lamentable answer: powerful gun lobbyists successfully defend the legal sale of "single-shot" assault rifles even as they are routinely smuggled into Mexico, where a simple tweak renders them fully automatic and ready to fire hundreds of rounds per minute in the hands of drug-cartel assassins.

Eighty percent of the 75,000 guns Mexican authorities seized from criminals during the past three years came from the U.S. This fact underscores the need to reclassify control of gun sales along our frontier as a matter of national security.

Putting the squeeze on the pipeline of money and weapons that feed Mexico's inferno would be the best Independence gift we could give Mexico. It would help more than any amount of guns, money, training and electronic spy data we might provide to Mexico's unreliable army and police.

Viewpoint

"Instead of succumbing to the siren call of legalization . . . , President Obama must ramp up U.S. support for President Calderón's fight against the cartels."

The United States Should Not Legalize Drugs but Should Support the Defeat of Drug Cartels

James Roberts

In the following viewpoint, James Roberts responds to an August 5, 2009, essay by Jorge Castañeda, a former Mexican Secretary of Foreign Affairs (2000–2003), in which he claims that America unfairly foists the burden of the drug war on Mexico's shoulders, even though the demand for drugs in the United States is driving this illicit business. Roberts replies by rejecting Castañeda's conclusion that legalization of drugs in the United States and Mexico would help rob the Mexican drug cartels of their power and wealth. He believes legalization would increase demand and lead to lawlessness in Mexico and America. Roberts insists that Mexico has to assume responsibility for harboring drug cartels and allowing narcotics from other Latin American countries to ship through Mexico's supply lines. He advocates that the United States resumes a hard-line stance on drug enforcement and gives as much aid to Mexico as it can to defeat the cartels. At the same time, Roberts maintains that Mexico's elite must support aggressive tactics to fight the cartels and stop passing the blame to the United States. Roberts is the research fellow in Freedom and Growth at the Center for International Trade and Economics at the Heritage Foundation, a conservative public policy think tank.

As you read, consider the following questions:

1. Which city's drug policy model shows, for Roberts, a failed attempt at resolving the problem of narcotics through legalization?

2. Why does the author contend that President Calderón has no choice but to use the Mexican army to fight the drug cartels?

3. What US drug policies endorsed by President Barack Obama does Roberts indicate are too soft and permissive to curb the problem of increasing demand?

With some artful sleight of hand, Professor [Jorge] Castañeda paints the United States into a corner politically and, as the elites in Mexico have done all too often in the past, points the finger of blame for Mexico's drug-related violence squarely at the Yankees [in an August 2009 essay]. He leaves open only the "easy" way out: legalization of psychotropic drugs in the United States. If we don't, the professor warns, we will face "the fire next door." Decriminalization or bust, so to speak. I beg to differ.

In fact, of all the potential solutions that Dr. Castañeda sets up and then knocks down, the decriminalization option is the least realistic politically and has the lowest probability of actually happening. Because notwithstanding the mixed signals the [Barack] Obama administration has sent about it since taking power, the American people know that legalization would be a disaster.

Mexico's Leaders Are Too Quick to Blame America for Mexico's Problems

Unfortunately former Foreign Minister Castañeda and others in the elites have tended to blame Mexico's domestic problems on the United States and then demand that the Americans fix them. When the "Mexican Miracle" fizzled out in the late 1970s, the elites should have reformed their outdated political and economic institutions. Instead, they exported their problem to the United States by encouraging massive out-migration and reaped a hard-currency windfall in remittances.

Professor Castañeda even finds a way to blame the current drug problem on Richard Nixon in 1969! Perhaps he forgets that was the watershed year when baby boomers virtually invented Nixon's "Silent Majority," who were alarmed as their children began toking up with "Proud Mary" from Mexico, rebelled against 200 years of the American Protestant work ethic, and trudged through the muddy fields of the socialist Woodstock Nation.

The Heritage Foundation's *Index of Economic Freedom* details pervasive corruption and weak rule of law stunting economic growth and job creation in Mexico. A recent Transparency International report found that many political leaders are neck-deep in drug-related corruption and concludes that this stain upon the country's honor cannot be seriously addressed until the elites reform themselves. President [Felipe] Calderón has been courageous in showing them the way.

Americans Will Never Permit the Legalization of Drugs

Dr. Castañeda's facile assumption that the Yankees will come to Mexico's rescue yet again by decriminalizing drugs, thereby putting the cartels out of business, minimizes the obstacles. Exactly how will U.S. politicians sell their constituents on this fundamental change—one that goes directly against the grain of American exceptionalism? As [President Bill] Clinton-era Drug Czar and retired General Barry McCaffrey stated emphatically in a talk at Heritage [Foundation], decriminalization will never happen in the United States because the American people will oppose the legal sale of substances that can destroy healthy bodies and so easily degrade the human spirit while increasing crime.

Six months ago budget-busting nationalized Obamacare [health care reform] and ruinously expensive, nontransparent "Cap-and-Trade" legislation [for carbon emissions] looked like sure bets to sail through the U.S. Congress. Not anymore. Decriminalization won't, either, because the American people know that legalization in places like crime-infested Amsterdam has failed just as miserably as has the fiscally unsustainable European social welfare model.

Decriminalization Would Create New Problems and Not Solve the Old Ones

The Heritage Foundation's Cully Stimson enumerates the many practical problems that decriminalization would create. Inevitably the government would control every aspect of legally available psychotropic drugs—their manufacture, importation, and sale. They would instantly become a magnet for corrupt officials.

Moreover, lawmakers faced with spiraling budget deficits would be sorely tempted to impose high "sin taxes" on these morally problematic products. Gray market incentives for criminals (viz cigarette smuggling) would engender the very same Prohibition-style violence that decriminalization advocates decry. If taxes miraculously remained low and "street" prices for the drugs dropped (no-risk premium), consumption would skyrocket and (more) violence and social disloca-tion would follow. We would end up right back where we started, but worse off.

A Network of International Drug Cartels Shipping Product Though Mexico

The international drug cartels are increasingly shipping their products from Venezuela through rapidly destabilizing Central American countries and into Mexico for overland smuggling into the United States. From [Afghani] Taliban *jihads* funded with opium profits to the trouble Hugo Chávez is stirring up in Colombia (via drug-trafficking FARC [Revolutionary Armed Forces of Colombia] guerillas) and elsewhere in the region, would-be totalitarian dictators bent on overthrowing democratic governments and undermining U.S. influence are working closely with narco-traffickers.

Gustavo Coronel, a Venezuelan expatriate and engineer who has studied the would-be president-for-life for years, notes that Chávez has cut ties with U.S. drug enforcement of-ficials and ordered Venezuelan government officials to cooper-ate with the drug cartels instead. Venezuela is now the princi-pal conduit for Andean cocaine going to the United States and Europe.

Using the immense cash flow generated by oil sales and narco-trafficking, Chávez has provided financing for extreme left presidential candidacies in Bolivia, Ecuador, Peru, El Sal-vador, and Nicaragua. Recent U.S. government reports tie an-other president-for-life wannabe, Manuel Zelaya of Honduras, to Chávez cocaine cash and trafficking. Chávez also reportedly helped to bankroll the campaign of leftist Andrés Manuel Lo-pez Obrador, who nearly won the Mexican presidency in 2006. Dr. Castañeda makes no mention of any of these very signifi-cant aspects of the current threat.

Stopping the Flow of Guns and Curbing the Demand for Drugs

The United States must do more to rally its own law enforcement community around a common strategy to be sure the various Washington agencies involved play their assigned roles. Specifically, the United States should use much of the remaining Mérida [Initiative] funding to help build the capacity of the Mexican federal and state police and develop a command-and-control center for intelligence sharing and communications. Washington should also improve its efforts to stanch the flow of weapons and cash across the United States' border into Mexico.... And as part of a longer-term effort, both nations, but especially the United States, should seek to reduce the domestic demand for drugs through education and treatment programs.

Robert C. Bonner, "The New Cocaine Cowboys,"
Foreign Affairs, *July/August 2010.*

The Rule of Law Is Failing in Mexico and America

Rule of law and security are under siege in North America from criminal organizations. Understandably, President Calderón and the Mexican people feel they are bearing a heavy burden in their fight to dismantle drug cartels and stop the flow of tons of cocaine, marijuana, heroin, and methamphetamines to the United States. Since 2006, more than 10,000 Mexicans have been murdered in drug-related killings, 600 of which were law enforcement and military personnel. Mexico's internal security and future governability are threatened by lawlessness.

Americans also feel increasingly victimized and powerless, however, as they watch their government struggling to control the chaos wrought by drug trafficking along the southern border. Mexican drug cartels aggressively push their destructive products on American consumers. They operate in 230 U.S. cities and are America's largest organized crime threat.

President Calderón has asked for and needs U.S. help. The [George W.] Bush administration's Mérida Initiative [a cooperative plan to train Mexican law enforcement and supply it with technology to fight the drug cartels] was modeled on the successful Plan Colombia. But implementation has been slow and the current size of the program is inadequate to the task at hand, as Professor Castañeda rightfully points out. The roadblocks, however, have been set up by his former ideological soul mates on the left. Some Democrats in Congress and leftist U.S. NGOs [nongovernmental organizations] want to block the assistance, claiming the Mexican military commits serious human rights violations. They seem to forget the human rights of the thousands of victims of drug violence.

Dr. Castañeda complains that Plan Colombia was "as much a counterinsurgency effort as a drug-enforcement program." Why is that a problem, professor? Where do you draw the line between the two threats? Why would we not want to see the same positive outcomes in Mexico through the Mérida Initiative? His answer boils down to four words: "Boots on the Ground."

Mexico's Narco-Insurgency Armies

Today two major cartels—Gulf and Sinaloa—battle each other for turf. [The College of] William & Mary political science and renowned expert on Mexican affairs Professor George Grayson calls the violence of the cartels "grotesquely brutal"; beheadings are commonplace. He tallied up their arsenals, which include AR-15 and AK-47 assault rifles (Chávez recently purchased 200,000 AK-47s from the Russians), MP5s and

50-mm machine guns, grenade launchers, ground-to-air missiles, dynamite, bazookas, and helicopters. None of these military-grade weapons could be obtained legally from the United States. Professor Castañeda repeats the media meme by alleging that, again, it's America's fault since the guns doing the killing in Mexico come from the United States.

In fact most of the conventional and military weapons come from third countries. Many have been stolen from Mexican army depots by the "Zetas," former Mexican army commandos gone bad.

Dr. Castañeda faults President Calderón for using the military to take on "all of the cartels, all the time." The reality is that Calderón has no choice; the survival of the Mexican state is at risk. The Mexican government is fighting a series of drug-funded mini-insurgencies for control of huge chunks of the national territory. In a recent report, General McCaffrey explained that the local police are outgunned and corrupted. Only the military can face the cartels and their platoon-sized units using night vision goggles, encrypted communications, sophisticated information operations, and sea-going submersibles. Professor Castañeda's lament that Chile and Colombia have organized effective police forces while Mexico has not only serves to highlight another failure of the Mexican elites to lead.

The United States Must Defend Mexico's Sovereignty

The Obama administration has sent disquieting and confusing signals about the direction of its drug policy. White House Drug Czar [Gil] Kerlikowske claims the "war on drugs" is over and that the administration is now waging a vaguely defined "war on a product" that emphasizes new drug-demand reduction and treatment options. Gone is the Bush administration's hard-line stance on enforcement, replaced by softer and more permissive policies that green-light "medical marijuana" and coddle users by promoting "needle exchanges."

Instead of succumbing to the siren call of legalization from Professor Castañeda and others, President Obama must ramp up U.S. support for President Calderón's fight against the cartels. Ironically, 160 years after the Mexican-American War, only the Americans have the capacity to help the Mexicans defeat the narco-terrorists and preserve their sovereignty. Active-duty, uniformed U.S. military help is not necessary—U.S. government civilians can give advice and training in addition to keeping track of sophisticated U.S. military equipment.

President Obama should also get personally involved in the U.S. demand-reduction effort by loudly and clearly voicing his personal opposition to drug consumption and abuse, and by speaking directly on the harm done, not only by trafficking, but also by consumption of illegal substances, including marijuana. This would significantly boost the effectiveness of demand-reduction messages at home and abroad and bring needed clarity to the president's stance on the issue.

Take a Stand for Truth, Justice, and the Mexican Way

Jorge Castañeda should oppose the wealthy and powerful forces that would enslave millions in lives lost to drug addiction and violence. Such bravery could even help him realize his dream of winning Mexico's presidency.

Dare to take a stand for the right thing in Mexico, professor, don't take the "easy" way out. Don't support the legal sanctioning of these physically and morally destructive drugs. Rally the center-left and leftist parties to support Calderón in his fight against the cartels. Be the one to finally say to the Mexican people and the elites, enough corruption!

Stand against the dark forces, professor, and prevail!

> "So, it doesn't appear that there is much
> that realistically can or will be done to
> help Mexico."

The United States Can Do Nothing to Help Mexico

Robert Robb

Robert Robb is an editorial columnist for the Arizona Republic. *In the following viewpoint, Robb traces the economic and political progress Mexico made during the 1990s only to point out how disastrous the current turn of events in that country has been. As Robb reports, the rule of law in Mexico has been subverted by political corruption and the rise of drug cartels. The Mexican government's fight against the cartels is causing too much friction with local communities, thus destabilizing the state. According to Robb, the United States has tried to offer aid but to little effect. Other US policies have similarly failed to assist Mexico. Robb concludes that Mexico may have to fight this battle on its own.*

As you read, consider the following questions:

1. In what year was Mexico admitted into the OECD, according to Robb?

2. As the author reports, what is the estimated value of the drug trade from Mexico to the United States?

3. What does Robb say would be the thing America could do to most help Mexico in its fight against the cartels?

M exico is a developing tragedy.

The country has an almost cursed history.

Born in conquest, the rule of law and the peaceful transition of power never took firm root after independence from Spain in 1821. The Institutional Revolutionary Party (PRI) provided a period of relative stability and peace after it consolidated power in 1929. But its corporatist economic policies stifled the productive capacity of the Mexican people and their resources.

Then, in the 1990s, Mexico appeared to have turned a corner.

After a currency crisis, Mexico got a handle on the art of sound money. Inflation abated and the peso began to retain its value, at a time when monetary instability still characterized much of Latin America.

Economic Growth and Free Elections

In 1994, Mexico was admitted into the Organisation for Economic Co-operation and Development [OECD], the 30 leading global industrialized economies. Mexico had, and still has, a per capita GDP [gross domestic product] of less than half the OECD average. Still, it was recognition that Mexico had at least begun to develop a modern industrialized capacity.

Then, the PRI eased its monopoly on political power, permitting a free and fair presidential election in 2000, which was won by Vicente Fox of the National Action Party (PAN). So Mexico had a peaceful transfer of power. Opposition parties retained control of the Mexican parliament, so Fox's economic reforms were largely stymied. Still, he was able to reduce the bureaucratic obstacles to business formation and started the process of moving Mexico's large informal economy into the open where it can be more productive. The *Economist* was writing about Mexico's emerging middle class.

However, the country had a cancer—the illegal drug trade. It was subverting the rule of law at the local level. Stable money and a favorable tax and regulatory climate are prerequisites for economic growth. So is the rule of law.

Fox began the battle to reduce the influence of the drug cartels. However, it has been greatly escalated by his successor, Felipe Calderón, elected in 2006. He has, in essence, declared war on the cartels.

A Failing War Against Drugs

The war does not appear to be going well. The influence and intimidation of the drug cartels on local governments and communities is increasing, not decreasing. To overcome the influence of the cartels at the local level, Calderón is fighting it with national forces and agencies. But the corruption has moved to those national agencies, and reports of abuses by the national drug-fighting forces are increasing, creating friction and tensions between local populations and the national government.

I don't know whether the fears that Mexico will become a failed state are warranted. But it is no longer a country that appears to have a brighter future, at least in the intermediate term.

America Cannot Help

So what, if anything, should the United States be doing about this?

The United States has substantially increased aid to Mexico to fight the illicit drug trade, pledging $1.4 billion through the Mérida Initiative [a cooperative plan to train Mexican law enforcement and supply it with technology to fight the drug cartels]. But the value of the drug trade from Mexico to the United States is huge, an estimated $15 billion to $25 billion a year.

The drug war in Mexico has become a battle of wills, in which financial assistance from the United States, in any amounts that are realistic, will have at best a marginal effect.

Some have proposed a Marshall Plan [the post–World War II economic plan to rebuild Europe] for economic development in Mexico. But Mexico's economy needs internal liberation, not foreign aid. Moreover, having better legal alternatives doesn't eliminate the allure of high illicit profits. Organized crime still exists in the United States.

What the United States could do that would most help Mexico would be to legalize marijuana, which provides 60 percent of the cartel's revenue. That might shrink the cartels to the point that the Mexican government could tame them. But there are obviously huge domestic considerations about doing that as well, and it is a policy initiative that remains beyond the foreseeable horizon.

So, it doesn't appear that there is much that realistically can or will be done to help Mexico. But this much can be observed: History owes the Mexican people a break.

Periodical Bibliography

The following articles have been selected to supplement the diverse views presented in this chapter.

John Antal	"Border Battles: The Future of Border Security Technology Along the US–Mexican Border," *Military Technology*, 2010.
Peter Baker	"On Foreign Policy, Obama Shifts, but Only a Bit," *New York Times*, April 17, 2009.
Jonathan Broder	"Drugs and Violence Too Close to Home," *CQ Weekly*, March 9, 2009.
Charlie Cook	"Our Neighbor's Drug Problem," *National Journal*, March 28, 2009.
Angelo M. Cordevilla	"Pro-Mexico," *American Spectator*, June 2009.
Economist	"Turning to the Gringos for Help," March 27, 2010.
Chris Hawley	"Mexico: Gun Controls Undermined by US," *USA Today*, April 1, 2009.
Elisabeth Malkin and Randal C. Archibold	"US Withholds Millions in Mexico Antidrug Aid," *New York Times*, September 4, 2010.
Rob Margetta	"A Drug War Surge," *CQ Weekly*, April 19, 2010.
Tim Padgett	"The Moment," *Time*, April 6, 2009.
Peter Schrag	"Blowback at the Border," *Nation*, May 4, 2009.

For Further Discussion

Chapter 1

1. After reading the viewpoint by Mario Loyola, list some of the ways in which he says drug cartels are destabilizing Mexico. In Loyola's opinion, how has the Mexican government failed to control the cartels? What evidence does he give that the Mexican government has made some progress in the fight?

2. Dudley Althaus asserts that efforts to clean up the Mexican law enforcement agencies have not successfully purged their ranks of pernicious influence from the drug cartels. Ken Ellingwood, on the other hand, describes some of the efforts the Mexican government has employed to counter that influence. After reading both viewpoints, give your opinion on how optimistic Mexico should be about combating corruption among police and other law enforcement officials.

3. Jeff Faux contends that the North American Free Trade Agreement (NAFTA) has facilitated criminal activity in Mexico and is promoting instability in the nation. Examine some of his reasons and explain whether you believe they are accurate. Then read some of the articles in chapter 2 and conclude whether you think NAFTA should continue to set the terms of trade between the United States and Mexico or whether the policy needs to be changed.

Chapter 2

1. The *Economist* advocates that NAFTA remain a vital part of cross-border trade among the United States, Canada, and Mexico. Anne Vigna, however, argues that NAFTA has

destroyed agricultural markets in Mexico and served only US interests. Whose opinion do you find more credible? Explain why.

2. The maquiladora system in Mexico is the subject of much debate. Some critics, like Mike Westfall, maintain that these factories are nothing more than sweatshops for US corporations. Joseph Heinzman Jr. and Gian Marco Valentini, though, believe the maquiladoras are making Mexico competitive in global markets and encouraging wage growth and higher employment rates. Given the evidence from these articles, do you believe the maquiladoras are helping Mexican laborers rise from poverty, or are they keeping Mexican workers locked in low-wage jobs?

3. In his condemnation of NAFTA, David Bacon claims the trade agreement is compelling low-wage Mexican workers to flee their own country after the destruction of the agricultural sector and other markets. Demetrios G. Papademetriou counters that NAFTA has little to do with emigration. He insists the lure of better pay and more jobs has always brought Mexican immigrants to the United States. After assessing both viewpoints, do you think it is fair to blame NAFTA for increased migration or are other, more significant, factors at play?

Chapter 3

1. The first two viewpoints in this chapter enumerate some of the costs to the United States and Mexico associated with the building and strengthening of a border fence. Describe some of the costs to both nations and then take your own stand on whether a border fence is worth maintaining. Address arguments in both viewpoints in explaining your own views.

2. Ben Conery and Jerry Seper claim that border violence is becoming a serious problem on both sides of the US-Mexican border. What kind of argument do they make to

establish this claim? Julianne Hing and Hatty Lee state that border violence is not as rampant as reporters like Conery and Seper suggest. What kind of argument do they make to refute that claim? Whose opinion do you find more convincing? Explain whether the type of argument employed has anything to do with your opinion on the matter.

3. Marisa Treviño poses the unique argument that US emigrants to Mexico can be accused of placing some of the same burdens on Mexico's welfare structure that Mexicans in the United States are accused of placing on the US welfare system. Do you think the significance of the "burden" is the same in both cases? Using this viewpoint and any others from the anthology, explain why or why not.

Chapter 4

1. Dave Gibson contends that the United States should employ military forces to secure the US-Mexican border. He argues that the drug cartels have military firepower in their arsenals and thus should be countered with US military force. Do you think militarizing the border is an appropriate solution to the problem of drug trafficking? What do you think would be the advantages or disadvantages of such a policy?

2. After reading the viewpoints by Armand Peschard-Sverdrup and Laura Carlsen, decide whether you think the Mérida Initiative is a worthwhile piece of cross-border diplomacy or whether the policy is an example of US intrusion in Mexican affairs. Use specific arguments from the viewpoints to support your claim.

3. Ted Lewis and many other critics suggest that the United States could more efficiently undermine the power of the Mexican drug cartels by legalizing marijuana—depriving the cartels of high profits—and restricting the sale of guns—reducing the cartels' firepower. Do you believe

these measures would help topple the cartels or limit their violence? Read James Roberts's viewpoint on this topic as well as any others you can find in print or on the Internet. Describe the costs to the United States and Mexico in enacting such policies and explain whether Lewis's plan is, in your opinion, worthwhile.

Organizations to Contact

The editors have compiled the following list of organizations concerned with the issues debated in this book. The descriptions are derived from materials provided by the organizations. All have publications or information available for interested readers. The list was compiled on the date of publication of the present volume; the information provided here may change. Be aware that many organizations take several weeks or longer to respond to inquiries, so allow as much time as possible.

American Enterprise Institute for Public Polic Research (AEI)

1150 Seventeenth Street NW, Washington, DC 20036
(202) 862-5800 • fax: (202) 862-7177
website: www.aei.org

The American Enterprise Institute for Public Policy Research (AEI) is a nonpartisan public policy organization that espouses the ideals of free enterprise, limited government, and a vigilant national defense. Within its foreign policy research area, AEI scholars have focused on improving the US-Mexican partnership and promoting democratic solidarity throughout Latin America. Recently the institute published the report *The Drug Fight in Mexico: Failure Is Not an Option*, which outlines the steps that must be taken to eradicate illegal drug trade in both the United States and Mexico. Additional AEI articles addressing US policy toward Mexico include "The Threat South of the Border," "Model Minority?" and "A War You Can Stop," with others available in the monthly magazine of AEI, the *American*.

American Immigration Control Foundation (AIC Foundation)

222 West Main Street, PO Box 525, Monterey, VA 24465

(540) 468-2022 • fax: (540) 468-2024
e-mail: aicfndn@htcnet.org
website: www.aicfoundation.com

Founded in 1983, the American Immigration Control (AIC) Foundation has worked for nearly thirty years to limit immigration into the United States by publishing books, pamphlets, and videos informing the public about the harmful consequences of high immigration levels. The organization is particularly concerned about illegal immigration across the Mexican border into the United States that it believes threatens the American rule of law and places unnecessary burden on the US economy and people. AIC Foundation publications are available for purchase on the organization's website.

Americas Program

Cerrade de Xolalpa 7-3, Colonia Tortuga
   Mexico
011-52-555-324-1201
e-mail: info@cipamericas.org
website: www.cipamericas.org

The Americas Program is a program sponsored by the Center for International Policy that addresses the environmental, security, economic, and social problems that have been obstacles to positive development and cooperation in the Western Hemisphere in the past. The program's mission is to improve relations between all countries of the Americas by promoting dialogue and understanding through its policy reports, issue briefs, political commentary, and educational materials. Articles addressing issues related to Mexico include "Cancun Agreement Succeeds in Meeting Low Expectations," "Challenges and Risks for the Mexican Armed Forces, National Security, and the Relationship with the United States," and "How Legalizing Marijuana Would Weaken Mexican Drug Cartels." These articles and others can be accessed on the Americas Program website.

Cato Institute

1000 Massachusetts Avenue NW
Washington, DC   20001-5403
(202) 842-0200 • fax: (202) 842-3490
website: www.cato.org

The Cato Institute, a public policy organization, seeks to promote government policy in accordance with the ideals of limited government, free markets, individual liberty, and peace. The organization has addressed issues related to Mexico such as the drug war, immigration, and the economy. The institute is critical of the US government's limited intervention in the current situation and suggests drug decriminalization as an alternative to the current inaction. Publications on these topics include "Mexico's Failed Drug War," "Drug Decriminalization Policy Pays Off," and "Mexican Migration, Legalization, and Assimilation." Additional articles on these and other topics may be found in the tri-annual publication *Cato Journal*, the quarterly *Cato's Letters*, and the bimonthly *Cato Policy Report*.

Center for Immigration Studies (CIS)

1522 K Street NW, Suite 820, Washington, DC   20005-1202
(202) 466-8185 • fax: (202) 466-8076
e-mail: center@cis.org
website: www.cis.org

An independent, nonpartisan think tank, the Center for Immigration Studies (CIS) researches the economic, social, and demographic impacts of immigration in the United States. The institute maintains that its view of immigration is both pro- and low-immigrant, arguing that allowing fewer immigrants into the country will benefit those admitted and US citizens alike. CIS believes that immigration should be controlled by stricter border security combined with immigration policy reform. Detailed information about CIS's position on the issue can be read in the backgrounders and reports, testimonies, and op-eds available on the organization's website.

Council on Foreign Relations (CFR)
The Harold Pratt House, 58 East Sixty-Eighth Street
New York, NY   10065
(212) 434-9400 • fax: (212) 434-9800
website: www.cfr.org

The Council on Foreign Relations (CFR) is a nonpartisan, membership organization that publishes non-biased public policy briefs about topics currently of interest in the United States. No official council position is ever given in these reports; however, individual scholars are given the opportunity to voice their beliefs in commentary pieces and at the conferences hosted by the organization. With regard to the current situation in Mexico and the role that should be taken by the United States, events such as "200 Years of US-Mexico Relations: Challenges for the 21st Century Symposium" and "Beyond NAFTA: Raising Cross-Border Competitiveness" offer opportunities for debate. Transcripts, audio, and video of these events can be accessed online along with additional articles and policy briefs concerning Mexico and US-Mexican relations. *Foreign Affairs* is the bimonthly publication of CFR.

Economic Policy Institute (EPI)
1333 H Street NW, Suite 300, East Tower
Washington, DC   20005-4707
(202) 775-8810 • fax: (202) 775-0819
e-mail: epi@epi.org
website: www.epi.org

The Economic Policy Institute (EPI) has been working since 1986 to provide a voice for low- and middle-income workers in national economic policy debates. While the institute focuses on US economic policy, much effort has also been dedicated to examining the relationship between American and Mexican economic policy decisions, particularly the impact of the North American Free Trade Agreement (NAFTA). Articles examining these issues include "Revisiting NAFTA: Still Not Working for North America's Workers," "South of the Border: The Impact of Mexico's Economic Woes," and "How NAFTA

Failed Mexico." These articles and others can be accessed on EPI's website, with additional information available in the institute's official publication, *EPI Journal.*

Federation for American Immigration Reform (FAIR)

25 Massachusetts Avenue NW, Suite 330
Washington, DC 20001
(877) 627-3247
website: www.fairus.org

The Federation for American Immigration Reform (FAIR) advocates for immigration reform that includes improved border security to halt illegal immigration and limited immigration levels as policies necessary to maintain the US economy and security. The organization examines the impact of both legal and illegal immigration on national security, societal issues, and population growth. Much of the organization's focus has centered on immigration across the US-Mexican border and its impact on US-Mexican relations, with topics such as corruption, drug violence, and remittances to Mexico. Articles detailing these issues can be read on FAIR's website.

Global Policy Forum (GPF)

777 UN Plaza, Suite 3D, New York, NY 10017
(212) 557-3161 • fax: (212) 557-3165
e-mail: gpf@globalpolicy.org
website: www.globalpolicy.org

The Global Policy Forum (GPF) works as an independent watchdog, monitoring the United Nations' actions and global policy making to ensure accountability, and focuses specifically on the United Nations Security Council, the food and hunger crisis, and the global economy. With regard to the global economy and trade between the United States and Mexico, GPF has critiqued the North American Free Trade Agreement (NAFTA) as insufficient alone as a development strategy and in need of reform. Further, the organization has emphasized the negative impact of NAFTA on workers. Articles detailing these opinions can be read on GPF's website.

Heritage Foundation

214 Massachusetts Avenue NE, Washington, DC 20002-4999
(202) 546-4400 • fax: (202) 546-8328
e-mail: info@heritage.org
website: www.heritage.org

The Heritage Foundation is a conservative organization that promotes government policies that align with ideals such as free enterprise, individual freedom, limited government, and a strong national defense. As such, the organization supports open borders and free trade while at the same time calling for improved border security through more vigilant and increased border patrol. Heritage scholars have recently criticized Mexico's tariffs on US imports to the country, encouraged US involvement to end the drug war, and defended NAFTA. The Heritage Foundation's website provides access to these articles and others concerning Mexico.

Office of the United States Trade Representative (USTR)

600 Seventeenth Street NW, Washington, DC 20508
(202) 395-6135 • fax: (202) 395-4549
website: www.ustr.gov

The Office of the United States Trade Representative (USTR) is the Executive Office of the President responsible for negotiating with foreign governments to enact trade agreements, address disputes, and play a part in global trade organizations. More than two hundred professionals with expertise in regions all over the world serve as ambassadors for US trade in these areas. The USTR's website provides extensive information about current US trade agreements including NAFTA. Information about trade between Mexico and the United States can be found on the website as well.

Social Science Research Council (SSRC)

One Pierrepont Plaza, 15th Floor, 300 Cadman Plaza West
Brooklyn, NY 11201
(212) 377-2700 • fax: (212) 377-2727

e-mail: info@ssrc.org
website: www.ssrc.org

The Social Science Research Council (SSRC) has been working since 1923 as an independent, nonprofit research organization addressing global social science issues. The four main program areas are global security and cooperation, knowledge institutions, migration, and renewing the public. SSRC has published numerous reports concerning a variety of issues facing Mexico today such as *The Effects of Migration on Child Health in Mexico*, *Electoral Competition and Institutional Change in Mexico*, and *Remittances, Inequality, and Poverty: Evidence from Rural Mexico*. These reports and others on topics such as immigration, economics, and politics can be accessed on SSRC's website.

United States Department of Homeland Security (DHS)
US Department of Homeland Security
Washington, DC   20528
(202) 282-8000
website: www.dhs.gov

The US Department of Homeland Security (DHS) is the government office responsible for ensuring that the country is secure by enacting plans that emphasize both prevention and preparedness. Additionally, this is the government agency charged with immigration services and US Customs and Border Protection (CBP), which is the law enforcement agency whose officers patrol and man the US borders to keep them physically secure. DHS's website offers information about current border programs such as the Secure Border Initiative as well as additional facts about customs and border protection.

Bibliography of Books

Peter Andreas   *Border Games: Policing the U.S.-Mexico Divide*. Ithaca, NY: Cornell University Press, 2009.

David Bacon   *The Children of NAFTA: Labor Wars on the U.S./Mexico Border*. Berkeley: University of California Press, 2004.

Charles Bowden   *Murder City: Ciudad Juárez and the Global Economy's New Killing Fields*. New York: Nation Books, 2010.

Maxwell A. Cameron and Brian W. Tomlin   *The Making of NAFTA: How the Deal Was Done*. Ithaca, NY: Cornell University Press, 2000.

Howard Campbell   *Drug War Zone: Frontline Dispatches from the Streets of El Paso and Juárez*. Austin: University of Texas Press, 2009.

Jerome R. Corsi   *The Late Great USA: NAFTA, the North American Union, and the Threat of a Coming Merger with Mexico and Canada*. Los Angeles: World Ahead Media, 2007.

David J. Danelo   *The Border: Exploring the U.S.-Mexican Divide*. Mechanicsburg, PA: Stackpole, 2008.

Alexander S. Dawson   *First World Dreams: Mexico Since 1989*. New York: Zed Books, 2006.

Emily
Edmonds-Poli
and David A.
Shirk

Contemporary Mexican Politics.
Lanham, MD: Rowman & Littlefield
Publishers, 2009.

Ken Ellingwood

*Hard Line: Life and Death on the
US-Mexico Border.* New York:
Vintage, 2005.

George W.
Grayson

*Mexico: Narco-Violence and a Failed
State?* New Brunswick, NJ:
Transaction, 2009.

Judith Adler
Hellman

*The World of Mexican Migrants: The
Rock and the Hard Place.* New York:
New Press, 2009.

Bill Ong Hing

*Ethical Borders: NAFTA,
Globalization, and Mexican Migration.*
Philadelphia: Temple University
Press, 2010.

Gilbert M. Joseph
and Timothy J.
Henderson

*The Mexico Reader: History, Culture,
Politics.* Durham, NC: Duke
University Press, 2002.

Daniel C. Levy
and Kathleen
Bruhn with
Emilio Zebadúa

*Mexico: The Struggle for Democratic
Development.* Berkeley: University of
California Press, 2006.

Douglas S.
Massey

*Beyond Smoke and Mirrors: Mexican
Immigration in an Era of Economic
Integration.* New York: Russell Sage
Foundation, 2003.

Ronald L. Mize and Alicia C.S. Swords — *Consuming Mexican Labor: From the Bracero Program to NAFTA*. Toronto, Canada: University of Toronto Press, 2011.

Martha A. Ojeda and Rosemary Hennessy — *NAFTA from Below: Maquiladora Workers, Farmers, and Indigenous Communities Speak Out on the Impact of Free Trade in Mexico*. Missouri City, TX: Coalition for Justice in the Maquiladoras, 2006.

Tony Payan — *The Three U.S.-Mexico Border Wars: Drugs, Immigration, and Homeland Security*. Westport, CT: Praeger Security International, 2006.

Julia Preston and Samuel Dillon — *Opening Mexico: The Making of a Democracy*. New York: Farrar, Straus and Giroux, 2004.

Agnes Gereben Schaefer, Benjamin Bahney, and K. Jack Riley — *Security in Mexico: Implications for U.S. Policy Options*. Santa Monica, CA: RAND, 2009.

Index

Housing
    inflated real estate, American
        immigrants, 174, 177–178
    maquiladora workers, 97–98
Human rights abuses
    border patrol and force, 170
    land use, border fence, 149
    Mexican army, in drug war,
        22, 72, 182, 200, 204, 206–
        207
    migrant workers in US, 123–
        124, 125
    NAFTA and agribusiness, 88
    NAFTA and maquiladora sys-
        tem, 77, 93–103
    political protest repression,
        118, 204–205
Human trafficking, 27–28, 41, 186

I

IBM, 95, 99
Identity cards, 156
Illegal immigration
    border militarization, 170,
        173, 184–188
    employers of undocumented
        workers, 114, 122, 123, 124,
        132–133, 150, 160
    fence/wall issue, 140–141,
        142–146, 147–151
    illegal American workers in
        Mexico, 178
    immigrant ages, 175
    Immigration Reform and
        Control Act effects, 114,
        132–133
    prison populations, 187, 190
    trends and totals, 119, 122,
        128, 133, 140, 152, 154, 158,
        159–160

US economy weakness, effects,
    152, 154, 158, 159
work and living conditions
    reasons, 101, 118, 119, 120–
    124
Immigration and emigration
    Americans burden Mexico,
        174–178
    border homicides, 170
    brain drain, 48
    history, cross-border employ-
        ment, 105–106, 120, 130–133
    legalization arguments, 123–
        124, 129, 132–133, 161
    NAFTA not responsible for
        increasing emigration, 126–
        137
    NAFTA promises and realities,
        68, 74, 91
    NAFTA responsible for in-
        creasing emigration, 112–125
    rates, 47, 91, 119, 131–132,
        132–133, 136, 152, 153–154,
        158, 160, 175
    reasons, 101, 112–125, 132,
        133, 137
    US economy discouraging
        immigration, 141, 152–157
    US economy hurt by
        immigrants' return to
        Mexico, 158–161
    See also Illegal immigration
Immigration and Nationality Act
    (1965 amendment), 131
Immigration reform, 114, 120,
    123–124, 132–133, 147, 149–151
Immigration Reform and Control
    Act (IRCA), 114, 120, 132–133
Incomes. *See* Wages
Indigenous populations, 17, 114,
    204–205